RESCUE TAILS

UNBREAKABLE BONDS BETWEEN DOGS & HUMANS

JULIANN BISTRANIN

GALLIVANT
PRESS

DEDICATION

To my co-workers and friends, who give so selflessly of your time and energy to make the lives of animals a little brighter and less lonely: your compassion is truly remarkable. The care you provide, often in the face of heartache, speaks to your unwavering dedication.

To my beloved dog, Jazzy:
I hope everyone has the chance to experience the kind of friendship and unconditional love you've given me.

In memory of my brother John and nephew Brian, who both lost their battles with cancer this past year. John always had a special bond with his dogs, bringing out their playful, quirky personalities with ease. Their joy reflected his.

CONTENTS

FOREWARD

An engaging, well-crafted, and lively narrative of pets and the people who adore them. Readers will laugh, cry, and fall in love with each heartwarming episode in this delightful book.
—Linda McClure

Julie Bistranin is truly a dog whisperer—when she speaks, dogs listen. Her stories are nothing short of captivating and extraordinary.
—John J. Knoernschild, *The Mind Garden Samurai*

INTRODUCTION

According to the ASPCA, 3.9 million dogs enter shelters across the country every year. Shelter workers face the daunting task of finding each of them a new home and a fresh start. Every dog has a story, a past, but once they entered the shelter, I tried to wipe the slate clean and offer them a new beginning.

I loved my job, and I loved every dog. Even when I walked into my office one day to find Max, a mischievous Labrador, devouring the peanut butter and jelly sandwich I'd brought for lunch and placed on top of my file cabinet, I couldn't help but laugh. I resigned myself to going hungry that day, but I still had to complain to him.

"I didn't steal your food, so why did you steal mine?"

I glanced at his full bowl in the middle of the floor. Still feeling unsatisfied, he sauntered over and began chomping on his dry, crunchy food. He looked up at me with those liquid brown eyes, ready to be friends again—how could I resist?

Another time, Sadie, a bored Border Collie, toilet-papered my office with a roll of poop bags.

"Sadie," I scolded, "look at this mess."

She didn't care. She wandered around, already looking for

her next project. How could I not laugh? Whether I was hungry or cleaning up after them, I always moved forward, getting to know each dog and discovering their inherent personalities. Some came from terrible situations, while others had simply lost their homes and families through unfortunate circumstances.

I had the job of helping them find new families or working opportunities where they could be loved and happy. After retiring, I decided to sit down and write the stories of some of the many dogs I had the pleasure of meeting—dogs given a second chance, whether as a welcomed family member or serving their community in some capacity.

When a book is finished, it's often signed "The End," but this book should be signed with "The Beginning." These are the stories of dogs who ended up in a shelter and found new beginnings.

I Call You Dog

*When God made the earth and sky, flowers and the trees,
He then made all the animals, the birds and the bees.*

When His work was finished, Not one was quite the same.

He said, "I'll walk this earth of mine and give you all a name."

*And so He travelled land and sea, and everywhere He went, a
little creature followed him until its strength was spent.*

*When all were named upon the earth and in the sky and sea,the
little creature said, "Dear Lord, there's not one left for me."*

*The Father smiled and softly said, "I've left you till the end, I'll
turn my own name back to front, and call you 'dog,' my friend."*

Author Unknown

THE GIFT

On a warm summer evening after work, Martie and I walked down to the old building to lock it up for the night. The old building is where we house dangerous dogs who are usually held by animal control. We had to make a last-minute check to ensure the safety of the dogs, lock the building, and set the alarms.

As we approached, we could hear the dogs barking, which was unusual because, by this time of evening, they were usually ready to settle down and go to sleep.

"Oh crap! There's a dog out," Martie said, pointing.

I looked through the fence to see a huge German Shepherd nervously running back and forth, trying to find his way out of the outdoor dog run. The outside runs have a narrow fenced-in walkway, which makes it easy for the staff to clean the outside kennels. Along the walk, there is another fence to prevent a dog from escaping onto the shelter property. Now, as we looked through the fence, we could see the loose Shepherd. This dog came to the shelter after biting two people without provocation and was now declared a dangerous dog. Somehow, we had to get him safely back into his kennel.

I suspected someone had left the padlock unlocked after the

morning cleaning. Shepherds are brilliant about studying things, and I knew he had worked on the gate until the padlock had dropped out. Next, he used his nose to lift the latch, and went out to the outside dog run surrounding the perimeter of the kennels. Thankfully, all the gates on the exterior fence were locked, but he would have escaped if given the chance. Seeing us, he ran back towards his kennel, growling and barking, not wanting us to come near him. We hoped he would run back inside, but that was where he had broken out of, and he had no intentions of going back.

He stood against the far fence, anxiously watching us and barking to warn us to keep away. We unlocked one of the outside gates, pushing it towards the fence to confine him to a smaller area. With less space to run in, he became more nervous and ran towards us, barking aggressively. Martie pushed on the gate with her body, holding it against the fence so he could not break through.

"Martie," I said, "stay behind this gate and try to distract him so I can run to the other side, go into the dog run, and open the gate to his kennel wider. Maybe he will run in, and I'll shut the gate behind him."

She looked at me apprehensively. "I don't think you should go in with him; there must be a better way."

"Well, we've got to get him back into his kennel somehow," I said. "Let's try this first."

As I left, I yelled back at her, "Keep talking to him, so his attention stays on you. When I'm ready, I'll call him. Stay put in case he comes back towards you, and if he hears me, shout so I have enough time to move away from him."

She nervously stood, pushing on the gate, talking to him while I ran around the corner to the other side, unlocking and entering the run. I tried to be quiet while handling the lock on the gate so I could get inside without him hearing me. I listened for Martie's yells, hoping the dog would not run back towards me.

Grabbing the gate to his kennel, I got behind it and pulled it towards me, holding it against the fence.

"Hey, hey, hey, come on pup, let's go, let's go," I yelled at the top of my voice.

I saw him charging around the corner toward me, growling and barking, but he stopped at the open gate to his kennel and would not go in.

Martie shouted, "Are you all right?"

"Yeah, but he won't go inside," I yelled back.

As soon as the dog heard Martie, he turned and ran back towards her, hurling himself against the gate, giving me time to get out of the dog run. I hurried back towards Martie while she stood, pushing hard against the Shepherd's onslaught. The Shepherd, now in a full rage, had the bottom part of the gate in his mouth, pulling determinedly as he tried to reach Martie. Martie's eyes were enormous with fright as she pushed hard against the gate.

"Do you think he would go into a large dog crate if we threw a treat into it, or maybe we should use the catch pole?" she asked, her voice trembling.

"I don't think a crate will work, but it's worth a try. Get the biggest crate you can find, and we'll try that first," I replied, taking her place behind the gate.

I knew the dog crate would not work, and I hated to use the catch pole unless it was absolutely necessary. I just wanted Martie's nervous, frightened energy out of there so I could have a few minutes to work with him. When she left, I stood there watching the Shepherd's body language. I spoke to him in a soothing voice to see if he would respond to me.

Soon, he stopped barking and began to relax. I knew he was frightened in these unfamiliar surroundings and actively looking for a way to escape. When he stopped growling and pacing, he moved to one side of the fence to watch me. His eyes softened as I continued to talk, and soon he yawned and sat down. Talking to him in a low, soft voice, I hoped he would feel more at ease and comfortable with me. Slowly, he laid down, front feet forward, tongue out, panting.

I opened the gate a crack, still talking to him. When he saw the gate move, he stood up and moved towards the opening, trying to push his nose through the space. I told him to wait, and he backed away. I waited a few minutes and then put my knee through the crack to see if he would show any aggression or charge at me. He came forward to smell my knee and again moved away, sitting back down. Relaxing more, he pushed back onto his haunches to lie down.

I continued to talk with him, moving my hands and body slowly. I was careful not to look at him with a hard stare, which might challenge him. When he gave me eye contact, I faked a yawn, and he yawned back at me, his tail thumping on the cement next to the gate. Relaxed, he placed his head down on his front legs, giving a huge sigh. I kept talking to him, my voice low and calm, soothing him, watching as his body became peaceful.

I could tell he felt comfortable with me until the silence was broken by Martie's frightened cries.

"What are you doing? He's going to bite you!"

The Shepherd jumped to his feet, growling and looking towards Martie. I held up my hand toward her with a stern look, warning her to be quiet.

"Shh, shh, shh," I whispered, getting the Shepherd's attention once again.

I talked to him, waiting for his body to relax and show signs of calmness. After a few minutes, he sat back down, watching me closely, his tongue out in a peaceful pant.

"You're scared, aren't you, my friend?" I said quietly. "I won't hurt you. You have nothing to fear from me. Would you like to go for a walk?"

As I spoke, he turned his head and listened attentively, his ears pricking forward in recognition. Then, lowering his body to the ground, he continued to move his tail back and forth in a friendly manner, yawning. Taking the loose leash from around my neck, I reached it in towards him so he could smell it. He pushed his head forward to sniff it, and I gently slipped the leash over his head. Without a negative reaction from him, I stepped into the run, knowing there was no going back now.

"Come on, boy, let's go for a walk," I said to him.

He stood up so we could walk down the run towards his kennel. I talked in the same calm voice while walking confidently beside him, never touching him. When we reached his kennel, we walked inside. Watching his body language closely, I carefully reached down, pulling the leash over his head.

"You're a good boy," I said quietly.

As I backed out of his kennel, closing the gate behind me, I padlocked it. During the whole incident, I felt no fear, but felt as if I was in a different realm. I had become a part of this dog's thinking, communicating to him I was his friend, part of a pack, and giving him permission to join it. I gave him deep respect, honoring him so I could earn his trust. Making it clear I was a friend, a leader, and that I was there to help him.

I had done this many times before—soothing under-socialized, frightened, or unpredictable dogs, and calming happy, energetic, and out-of-control dogs. I named it "Dancing with the Dogs" to reflect my deep connection with their thoughts and their reality.

Martie came running around the corner. "Crap! I can't believe you did that!" she yelled, waving her arms at me. "He has bitten two other people and has acted viciously since he came in. Either you're the bravest person I have ever met, or the craziest. Crap!" she exclaimed.

She stood there looking at me with wide eyes and blurted out, "Weren't you scared? I can't believe you did that!"

"No," I told her. "His body language told me he would not bite me."

I could have tried to explain to her what this Shepherd was feeling and why he did not bite, or how I communicated with him, but people rarely understood. Would he have bitten? Yes, without a doubt he would have bitten Martie because her energy was too high and nervous, and she felt fear. For the same reason, he might have harmed the person who entered the yard the next morning to clean, because they would have been fearful of seeing him loose. But with a confident person who was reading his body language and respecting him, that person he would respect, and he did.

I was born with "The Gift." My gift is being able to read and communicate with animals. I have always felt more comfortable in the animal world, where they do things out of instinct. Animals possess a pure innocence because of their freedom from the corrupt human mind.

As a child growing up, my grandfather noticed how animals reacted to me and watched me with a knowing smile. From the time I was a small child, I filled our home with every kind of animal my parents would allow in. Everything from ducks to a racehorse followed me home. I did not realize this was uncommon because animals were always a part of my life, and I was a part of their world.

My grandfather had 'The Gift' with horses. Growing up in Montana, he used his gift often. During World War I, they sent him to France, where he served as a corporal in the 81st Infantry Regiment. He served in the Meuse-Argonne campaign, covering the western front. In the war, they used draft horses to pull the caissons conveying the ammunition and gun artillery. In the early stages of the offensive, a violent battle broke out accompanied by heavy shelling. The troops did not have time to care for the horses, so dropping the tugs, they loosened the neck yokes and cut the lines, letting the horses run free in full harness.

During the night, artillery shells were landing all around them, with men jumping into shell holes on the battlefield to take cover. My grandfather, with two other soldiers, took cover in one of those massive shell holes. When early morning dawned, it was cold and foggy, with a mist eerily creeping along the ground. Strangely quiet after the night's battle, there were only the moans of injured men and the screams of frightened and hurt horses.

Grandpa crawled to the top of the shell hole, looking out over the burned, smoking battlefield, trying to locate the horses he could hear. They screamed and whinnied with fear, frightened by the battle that had erupted around them the previous night. The innocent animals, sent into battle with shells and gunfire exploding all around them. They smelled the smoke and blood, heard the artillery explode everywhere, and felt bullets whizz by, piercing their eardrums or hitting and wounding them. There was no place to run; their world had become an Armageddon—a war that was not theirs. Now their screams stretched out across the battlefield, reaching my grandfather's ears as they cried for help.

Hearing their cries, he crawled out of the shell hole onto the decimated battlefield. Laying with his face to the ground, he hoped the enemy had retreated and was no longer a threat so he would not get shot. Slowly, he stood, ducking and dodging as he sprinted towards the horses. When he came close to a horse, he stopped, and in a low, quiet voice, talked to him, clicking his tongue as he walked slowly towards him. With the comforting, familiar sound of a human voice, the horse calmed and did not bolt away from him. Reaching out, he touched his muzzle, smoothed his hands along his neck, and grabbed his mane. Next, he gently ran his other hand along the trembling horse's body, feeling for any signs of injuries. When the horse was calm, submitting to his touch, he swung up on his back.

Riding over the battlefield, he talked in a reassuring voice to the other frightened horses. He knew they would follow another horse, and he could lead them to safety. Throughout the predawn morning, he rounded up horses, bringing them back to camp to be fed, watered, and curried. Compassionate care was given to the horses, addressing both their physical and emotional wounds.

Later in the day, he went back out onto the battlefield to check on the injured horses lying on the cold ground. Horses too wounded to get up. Heartbroken, and with tears running down his cheeks, he shot the suffering horses who would not recover from their wounds, releasing them from their pain and fear so they would not have to die slow deaths. He did this until all that remained on the battlefield were dead men killed the night before and the dead horses. The battlefield, stained with red, served as a grim reminder of innocent lives lost, caused by evil men and their lust for power and war.

When you have this gift, it can be a privilege or a deep burden as you watch, touch, and interact with the innocent. You become a part of the happiness and joy or the screams and fears in the lives of an animal. As you watch and learn their body language, recognizing their needs, you hear their calls. You learn to synchronize to their movements, to dance in their world, and use the gift to help the helpless.

When I went to work for the shelter, I would try to explain to our director what was going on with the dogs. Before she knew me well and trusted me, she would say, "You don't know what this dog is feeling."

But she was wrong. I did know, and as the years went by, she observed the gift at work as I handled and evaluated the dogs. If I could, I would give the gift to others, but I cannot. After working at the shelter and observing people around animals, I learned and realized that even though they felt compassion and empathy, loving the dogs in their care, they did not hear, see, or feel what I experienced when I worked with dogs. They took great care of them, but they could not feel the behavioral needs the dogs were having. Many people learn to train and are excellent trainers, but the best trainers I have ever met are the ones who can read canine behavior.

When people watch me work with dogs, they often ask where I got my training, where I went to school, or why the dogs respond so well to me. For a long time, I did not know how to answer them, but finally, I learned to smile and say, "It is a gift."

"Your talent is God's gift to you. What you do with it is your gift back to God."

LEO BUSCAGLIA

BUTTERCUP

Members of my staff came running to my office one warm spring day in May, asking for help. They were trying to get a dog out of her kennel so they could clean it. They reported the dog was exhibiting aggressive behavior and trying to bite them. I grabbed a loose leash and walked toward the kennel area where we keep the dogs. Kevin was waving me down.

"She's not in there!" he told me, with a frustrated look on his face.

"She's in the small dog kennels."

I rounded the corner to see three people huddled together in fear. On the other side of the glass was a petite, golden-colored Pomeranian, weighing around three pounds. Even though she was tiny, she was fearless, dominating them with her barking and growls, displaying all her teeth in her foxy-looking face. She stamped her tiny feet at them, trying to drive them away. She was mad and holding her ground, keeping them at bay. Her little white weapons flashed, warning them she would bite. Poms, true to their breed, are unfriendly with strangers, and this little dog was no exception, showing indignation and refusing to tolerate any nonsense. As I approached the glass, she showed her teeth, yapping as she ran towards me.

"What is her name?" I asked, reaching for a towel.

"Buttercup," they spoke in unison.

"Buttercup!" I said in surprise, laughing. "Well, it doesn't fit her at this moment."

The kennels in the small dog area were five by five feet long and wide. The builders constructed the kennels with cement, elevated off the ground at a table-top level. Because the doors and front of the kennels were glass, people could look inside. Puppies, with their happy, playful temperament, would jump on the glass, excited to see people as they walked into the room. However, adult dogs who usually see people from floor level would become unnerved. They reacted by barking, growling, or acting aggressively. If they felt overwhelmed and frightened, they would lie in the corner on their beds, trying to hide from the strangers invading their space. If a dog did not want to come out of the kennel, staff would have to climb up into the kennel to reach them. As I crawled inside, Buttercup's barking became a high crescendo. She ran towards me, stomping her feet. Talking quietly to her, I slowly unfolded the towel, pushing her into a corner where I could gently lay it over her. Reaching down, I carefully picked her up. She struggled, whipping her head back and forth, trying to bite me.

"Boy, you are feisty," I said.

I held her tight next to my body while Kevin set a crate down and opened the door. Leaning over, I gently set her in front of it, and she shot inside, trying to get away from me. Kevin quickly shut the door behind her.

"I think she will settle in a few days," I said. "If you have to pick her up, use a towel. The carrier will be the safest place for her if she will go into it."

I picked up the crate to leave and told everyone I would take her to my office so they could clean. I knew it would be less stressful for Buttercup inside my office. There she would have some quiet time away from all the activity. I set the crate down on the office floor, turning it so she could see me. She turned around twice to lie down, relieved to have a quiet place to hide. While I worked at my desk, or if I moved around the room, I could hear her growls vibrating out of the carrier. When the morning crew finished cleaning, Kevin came in to get Buttercup.

Lifting the kennel, he looked in. "I wish she could understand we are not trying to hurt her."

"It will take her some time," I replied. "Put the crate into her kennel and keep the door open so she has a safe place to hide."

We both looked in the crate while Buttercup showed us her teeth.

"Once she learns to trust us, she will become friendly. It will have to be at her pace."

While looking at her, Kevin said, "Hey Buttercup! We just want to be your friends."

Deep from the recesses of her crate, I heard Buttercup give a warning growl.

"She's just mad," I said. "She will soon become a happier dog."

Well, that was an understatement because Buttercup stood her ground for weeks with no intention of becoming a cheerful dog or a bosom buddy with any of us.

Once I read through her documents, I discovered someone had brought Buttercup to the shelter and claimed her owner had left her with them for a month because of a family emergency. When she did not return for her dog, the person became concerned and tried calling her, leaving several messages. Her friend never returned the calls, so now she felt her friend had abandoned the dog. She was completing college in a week and planning to move to another state for a new job. Since she did not own the dog and found it difficult to handle, she did not want to bring it along. Even though she felt bad, she said she didn't know what else to do but bring her to the shelter for adoption.

The dog's name was Buttercup. She was spayed and approximately three years old. On Buttercup's paperwork, we wrote the owner's information she shared with us. We received a note from our director stating that we would hold the dog for two weeks while we attempted to reach the owner. If she didn't respond, we would start accepting applications and find a new owner for her.

I continued to bring Buttercup into my office every morning while the staff was cleaning. After a couple of days, I placed some wet food in front of her crate, opening the door. Smelling the food, she cautiously crept out and started eating. I sat watching her, hoping she would relax, but when I moved, she shot back into the crate, barking ferociously.

"I will wait you out, my friend," I said.

This went on for a couple of weeks before I had a breakthrough. One morning when I walked into the small dog area, she got off her bed wagging her tail. When I unlocked her kennel door, she ran into her crate to hide.

"This is tail-wagging progress," I thought happily, closing the door behind her.

Later in the day, we made more progress when she bravely took a treat from my outstretched hand. Two days later, while working at my desk, she came out of her crate, stretched, and sat up on her hind legs, begging. For the first time, I could put a slip lead over her head without her resisting. With her now leashed, we went outdoors for a walk, which she seemed to enjoy. Her walks became a part of her morning routine while the crew cleaned. She walked beside me jauntily, her head high, ears forward, prancing on her front feet.

I dubbed our walks "Buttercup's Promenade."

When we returned to my office, I had to be careful in taking the leash off because, depending on her mood, she might whip around on me to let me know that even though she was starting to like me, I was not to touch her. If she did this, I would use a towel so I could safely pick her up to slip the leash off. As the days passed, she began to trust me more when I handled her, but I still respected her and had to watch her closely because at times she would lift her lips, showing her teeth, warning me. On those occasions, I called her "Miss Spunky."

I knew she could adjust to a home if the owners would be patient and allow her time to get used to them.

Buttercup seemed happier and more content as time passed, but only in my office or during walks. She was a picky girl, only permitting a few people to handle her. If she did not know a new person and felt threatened when they came too close to her kennel, she would run into her crate, barking, trying to hide.

My director loved singing, and I could hear her sing, or hum as she walked the halls. If it was a gloomy day outdoors, it seemed to affect her mood because she hummed less. On one particularly warm, sunny day, I could hear her humming toward my office door.

Knocking, she came in. "How is Buttercup doing?"

I looked inside the crate she was now hiding in. "Buttercup has made significant progress," I told her. "But I think it will take a lot of time for her to adapt to a new home."

"Her new people will have to be very patient with her," I added.

"I may have a home for her," my director said, smiling. "They are Pom people and have owned them for years. They emailed me this morning wanting to know if she was available for adoption. I told them although she was initially cranky and unhappy, she's doing better now."

She bent over to look in the crate while Buttercup growled at her.

"I told them she might be a one-person dog."

Sitting back in my chair, I replied, "This may be a suitable home for her. I know she will be much happier out of the shelter environment."

She stood up to leave. "I'll call them back this afternoon to see if they are still interested and ask if they want to adopt her. If they do, I will set up an appointment for them to come and meet her."

Upon my return to the shelter after a weekend off, I was surprised to learn someone had adopted Buttercup. The girls eagerly told me the new owners were elderly, had experience with Poms, and had owned them in the past. They knew Buttercup would require time to settle in and were prepared to be patient. The staff was dancing with joy at the prospect that they would not have to put up with her cantankerous behavior. They raved about the new owners, ending the conversation by telling me they had renamed her Sophie.

Pat, always the realistic one, said in her pragmatic voice, "That was like adopting the Tasmanian devil out! I think it is just a matter of time before they bring her back because she is just plain cranky."

We all laughed, but deep down, we knew Pat might be right. It was all going to depend on the adopters. Could they be patient enough to wait out Buttercup's curmudgeon behavior? I hoped so. I wanted this to be a happy ending for her. Still, I felt a little sad I didn't get to say goodbye to her.

It did not take long for Pat's prophecy to come true. Two weeks after Buttercup's adoption, her new owners called, telling us they were going to bring her back. When they arrived at the shelter, they told us Buttercup, now Sophie, hated them. She growled or barked if they came near her and ran away, refusing to let her touch her. She stayed in her crate all day, coming out only to use her potty pad or eat. They had spent money on all kinds of treats, even resorting to pieces of hamburger, trying to win her affections.

With a sad look, the woman told me, "I'm convinced this dog has been abused, and I wonder if she will ever make a good pet." She teared up as she looked into Buttercup's crate.

"I have never been unsuccessful with a dog before, but we don't know what else to do. She's so unhappy."

Unhappy was the perfect word, so while the staff completed the surrender, I picked up her crate and took her to my office. She stayed inside her carrier most of the day, but eventually, she poked her head out to look around. She did a full stretch with her rear end in the air and pranced over to me, wagging her tail.

"Oh, I know your type," I said, reaching down to pet her.

I ran my hand over her soft head and down her back. She yawned, stretched again, and sat up on her hind legs, waving her front feet at me, begging for a treat.

"You are such a brat!" I scolded her. "That could have been a nice home for you."

Reaching into the treat bag, I gave her a treat.

"I should not reward you for your naughty behavior."

"What is with you? Didn't you like your new name?" I petted her some more.

"Well, you're back to Buttercup again."

She yipped at me, still begging, then for the first time, she jumped into my lap.

"No, my friend!" I said, scratching her behind her ears. "I will not take you home."

She turned her little body around in a circle and lay down. Later, I reached over, picking up the phone, asking my director to come look in my office window. When she looked in, I pointed to my lap where Buttercup was curled up, soundly sleeping. Soon, she had the rest of the staff crowded around my office window, looking in.

She whispered to them, "See, she can be nice! It just takes the right person."

"I'm not taking her home," I yelled, waking Buttercup up.

Once my director had seen that Buttercup could adjust, she decided she needed to go into foster care. Thinking she knew the perfect person to foster her. Small dogs were her specialty, and she had successfully fostered difficult ones for us before. She worked some kind of magic with them, and after being in her home for a time, they would come back to the shelter well-adjusted and ready to be placed in their new homes. Lila came to the shelter the next day to meet Buttercup.

"Wow! She is so tiny," she said, looking into her crate.

"How long did it take you to make up with her?"

"About a month," I said. It was only after she was adopted and then returned that I formed a connection with her.

Buttercup had bolted into her crate the minute Lila had entered the room.

She sat looking into Buttercup's carrier. "Well, I am retired and patient. I have all the time in the world to win her affection. I will wait her out." She smiled.

Not only was Lila patient, but she was the kindest person I had ever met. The dogs read her energy and trusted her as she worked her charms on them. I knew Buttercup would be a challenge for her, but I also knew if anyone could bring her around, it would be Lila. When they were ready to leave and walking towards the front door, we could hear Buttercup protesting with loud growls from the interior of her crate.

Lila called the first week to tell us Buttercup was still very unhappy, spending most of her time inside her carrier, but with a cheerful voice, she claimed, "I'm not giving up, and have resorted to tempting her with fresh meat."

Two weeks later, she called again to tell us Buttercup was making progress. More weeks passed, and then we received an email with pictures of a happy Buttercup curled up in a tight ball, contentedly sleeping beside Lila on her bed. As the time approached for her to be returned to the shelter, we made preparations for her adoption.

A few days before we put her on the website, Lila emailed, asking if we would consider adopting Buttercup to her. She told our director Buttercup would have a hard time adjusting to another home because it took her so long to trust anyone new. She told her she was in love with her and would love to keep her. Our director gladly agreed it would be a wonderful placement and approved the adoption. Lila came to the shelter the next morning with her on a leash to complete the adoption. We tried to give Buttercup attention and pet her, but she turned into her old grumpy self, showing her teeth and barking.

When they left, Pat said, "I wonder how many times Buttercup has tried to bite her."

"Well, we won't ever know," I said, watching the car drive away. "Because Lila would never tell us."

We knew Buttercup was now in a suitable home, and Lila would love her even if she was cranky.

Warm, sunny days marked the transition from summer to a golden autumn. I adore autumn, as the leaves transform into vibrant shades of red, orange, and yellow, swirling in the wind. We were all relieved we had heard no news about Buttercup when, late one afternoon, my director knocked on my office door.

"You will not believe this!" she said, looking puzzled. "There is a young woman named Junko at the front desk claiming she is Buttercup's owner and wondering if her dog is still here."

"What?" I said. "Where has she been all this time?"

Sighing, she said, "In Japan! When the tsunami happened in March, she left Buttercup with her friend to fly home to find her parents. She just returned to the States."

I sat back in my chair. "Wow! Why didn't she call her friend?"

"It took her weeks to locate her family, and there was no phone service. By the time she called, her friend had brought Buttercup to the shelter."

Shaking my head, I said, "Well, why didn't she call the shelter?"

My director shook her head. "I don't know, but I'm going to call Lila and tell her the situation. I know she has fallen in love with Buttercup, but I think under the circumstances we should try to resolve this in a fair way."

I looked at her, feeling a little apprehensive, but I knew she was right.

She stood up to leave. "I will talk some more with Junko and then call Lila to tell her what has happened."

She was not humming as she walked down the hall. Before leaving to go home, I stepped into her office to see what was going to happen.

Sadly, she said, "Lila is coming in tomorrow with Buttercup to meet Junko. She feels Buttercup should be the one to choose who she wants to be with. She told me if Junko is Buttercup's owner, she should have her back."

Junko came into the shelter early the next day and sat quietly in a chair by the front desk, waiting. It looked as if she had carefully dressed for this reunion with nice jeans and an orange sweater matching the falling leaves outdoors. Her long black hair was in a ponytail, giving her a childlike look. At eleven, Lila walked through the shelter doors with Buttercup on a leash. Junko leaned over to look at them, and with a quiet sob, she called Buttercup's name. Buttercup stopped, unsure at first, and then exploded into wild cries, pulling the leash from Lila's hand. She ran to Junko, jumping into her lap. Wagging her tail, she licked Junko on the face, whining in delight. She was overjoyed, wiggling all over as big tears ran down Junko's cheeks, dropping onto Buttercup's soft fur.

We had never seen this behavior from Buttercup and knew Junko was her owner. We introduced Junko to Lila, and they reached out to hug each other with Buttercup squeezed between them, one in sorrow, the other in sheer joy at finding her dog. They visited, sharing phone numbers, pictures, and stories about Buttercup. As the time approached for the visit to end, Lila knew Buttercup should go home with Junko. Junko cried with relief when she realized Lila was returning her. She embraced and thanked her for taking care of her dog, picking her up to leave. When they walked out the doors, Junko turned to wave, and we all stood beside Lila, as she bravely waved back, watching Buttercup leave with her rightful owner.

The tsunami affected countless individuals and animals in Japan on March 11, 2011, with many being displaced, left homeless, or losing their lives. People all over the world flew to Japan to find their loved ones. Hoping for someone to take care of them, they left their pets behind, with the expectation of being reunited upon their return. I wonder how many Buttercups there were and how many found their owners again, or did they end up in shelters like ours? World disasters affect so many people and pets; it even affected one little dog in our corner of the world. I hope they all had happy endings like Buttercup and somehow found their owners.

We did not hear from Lila until December, when she called to tell us she would drop off Christmas cookies with her homemade fudge. She did this every year, and we drooled in anticipation, waiting for a sugar feast. It was snowing lightly when she walked through the doors wearing a Santa hat with a basket on each arm.

Setting them on the front desk, she smiled. "Open this one first."

We opened it to see her decorated cookies surrounded by red

and green cellophane. Each of us picked out our favorite cookie, enjoying its rich flavors. I looked over at the other basket.

"That must be your delicious fudge."

Reaching down, I opened the basket, and out popped a little golden Pomeranian puppy with a red Christmas bow. We all laughed in delight as I picked the puppy out of the basket, holding her up to admire her tiny, soft cuteness. Emmi reached out to take her from me.

"How charming are you?" she said, petting her.

"Junko gave her to me for Christmas," Lila said. "Isn't she adorable?" Emmi handed her back to me. "What did you name her?"

Lila reached over to take her from me, lifting her to look into her cute, foxy face. "Honey, because she is so sweet," she said, smiling.

Glancing at our director, she pointed at one of the baskets. "There's a card in there for you to open."

Our director looked in the basket, retrieving a card.

Opening it, she read, "With gratitude, our family is donating to your shelter for the amazing care you provided to Buttercup and for reuniting her with our daughter. Sincerely, Junko's family."

She laid the card down and turned the check around for us to see the large donation they had given. We were thrilled by this unexpected gift, knowing their generous act would support us in caring for the animals who would arrive at our facility in the upcoming year.

Pat looked at Lila. "Do you miss Buttercup?"

Lila kissed her new puppy on the nose. "Yes, but when I remember Buttercup's reaction at seeing Junko, well, who couldn't be happy for them both?"

Hugging Honey close to her, she turned her for us to admire. "Just look at this happy little face. I think I got the better end of the deal, didn't I?"

As I stood there eating another Christmas cookie, celebrating the wonderful gifts we had all received, I watched Lila, admiring her new puppy. I knew Buttercup and Junko had a very happy ending, but Lila—well, she got the better end of the deal.

"The bond with a true dog is as lasting as the ties of this earth will ever be."

KONRAD LORENZ

CLAYTON

A utility truck drove into the shelter parking lot on a cold, windy November afternoon. The driver approached the front desk to ask if the shelter could help him with a dog he had found in the woods. He explained he had been working on power lines in the upper county and, while driving on the forest access road, noticed an animal lying in the ditch. He stopped to investigate and found a dog who appeared very starved and sick.

He called his company to report the dog and ask for permission to take it to a vet. They told him he could not put an animal in a company truck and advised him to call the county animal shelter. He looked up the shelter's number and left a message on their answering machine. Knowing he had to continue with his work, he poured some warm leftover soup from his thermos into his hard hat and left it beside the dog.

As he continued his work, he periodically checked his phone to see if the shelter had responded. When his day ended, he could not stop thinking about the dog. Driving back down the road, he saw the dog was still lying in the weeds.

Upset about having to leave the dog behind, he tied orange

ribbons on each fence and gate as route markers. When he reached the end of the road and turned onto the main highway, he pulled over and wrote the milepost number. He checked his phone again, but there was still no response from the shelter. Dialing their number again, he left another message, emphasizing it was an emergency and asking them to call him back.

Putting the truck into gear, he drove away. It was thirty-eight miles to the freeway, thirty-eight miles of worrying and stressing about the dog he had left without help. The thought troubled him, and he doubted whether the shelter had received his message.

He pulled over to the side of the road and, for the third time, placed a call, only to hear the same irritating voicemail. Frustrated, he threw his phone down on the seat beside him, feeling miserable for leaving the dog out there. He struggled with what to do and knew he had to get the dog help. Grabbing his phone, he typed in the shelter's address and wrote it down. Then, shifting his truck into reverse, he turned around to head towards the shelter.

He walked into the shelter forty-five minutes later, looking for someone to help him. Leaning over the front counter, the blue in his plaid shirt reflected the blue of his frustrated eyes as he told the director about the abandoned dog he had found in the woods. He explained that because of company rules; he could not take the dog to a vet or bring him to the shelter.

"I tried calling three different times with no response from you," he said, annoyed.

The director looked at the man with sympathy. "I'm so sorry. Our phones have been out all day. How can we help you now that you're here?"

"Someone needs to go get that dog," he said wearily. You can find him approximately 38 miles away on Highway 20, heading towards the town of Concrete. After turning onto the forest access road, you will drive another mile until you come to a closed gate. From there, you will drive about a third of a mile. The dog will be lying in some weeds on the left-hand side of the road. I have tied orange ribbons on the gate and fences to make it easier to find him."

Looking at the director, he pushed his hat away from his worried forehead.

"I cannot get the dog out of my mind, and in good conscience, I can't leave him out there to die, so I drove out here hoping I would find someone to help him."

The director assured him she would immediately send staff out to find the dog and picked up her phone to text Emmi, asking her to come to the front desk.

"I will leave directions for you," the man said with relief in his voice.

After writing them out, he handed them to the director and turned to leave. When he reached the door, he turned back to give her one last look. "I wrote my name and phone number," he said, pointing at the paper he had handed her. "No matter what the outcome is, I would like to know, so please call me if you find him?"

"Yes," the director assured him as she looked down at the paper. "We will call and let you know. Thank you, Mr. Clayton, for driving out here. I'm sorry you had to go to all this trouble, but I'm glad you did. It shows what a kind person you are, and I'm sending people out to find the dog as soon as they can get ready."

Emmi was zipping up her coat as she entered the office, and I could tell she was on a mission. I loved working with Emmi because she has such a calm, quiet personality. When working together, we were a skilled and proficient team, synchronized in thought as we planned how to safely and carefully handle animals who needed our help.

While pulling her hat down over her head, she asked, "Would you be willing to go with me to find a sick dog out in the woods?"

She told me the dog was in the upper county, and it would take a while for us to find him. I put on my hat and coat while she ran to get the van. I told her I would gather what we needed to take with us. I hurriedly grabbed a large kennel, leash, dog food, and blankets, and when I was ready to leave, I met her outside.

We loaded everything into the van, and as we pulled out of the shelter parking lot, it was three o'clock in the afternoon. Our concern grew, as we knew we would lose daylight soon. We turned onto Highway 20, with our destination being a sick dog.

After driving thirty-eight miles on the highway, we spotted the milepost number, and a few yards further, we spotted one of the orange ribbons fluttering in the breeze. Turning off the main road, we drove deep into the woods until we reached a wire gate with more orange ribbons tied to it. I shivered in the damp, penetrating November air as I got out to open the gate, dragging it to the side of the road.

Getting back into the warmth of the van, I told Emmi we would leave it open for now and close it when we came back through. The woods were thick with a heavy, cold mist, which twisted its way through the trees, sending long, ghostly fingers along the ground. Driving deeper into the woods, we watched closely for the man's yellow hard hat he had left behind with the dog.

"Do you see anything?Emmi asked, gripping the steering wheel tightly as she leaned forward to get a better view.

I shook my head as I leaned forward, staring out the windshield, trying to see through the eerie mist that was enclosing us. Finally, Emmi spotted the hat, and a few yards away, we could see the dog lying in the tall weeds. Stopping the van, we jumped out onto the cold and frosty ground and walked toward the dog.

We both worried he might have already died, but as Emmi bent down next to him, he lifted his head off the ground to look at us. He was skeletal, missing most of his hair and his bare skin covered in mud. Talking softly, we reached out to pet him, but he growled, trying to crawl away from us. Dragging himself further away, he tried to stand but, exhausted, fell back onto the ground.

"Oh, my God!" Emmi moaned. "He's missing a leg."

I looked closely and saw he was missing his back left leg.

"Get the kennel out of the van," Emmi said. "I don't think he is going to let us handle him."

I ran to the van, pulled the kennel out, and dragged it close to where he was lying. We could see he did not have a collar on, so I made a loop with the leash. Reaching down, I tried to place it around his neck, but he snapped at me.

"How are we going to get him into the kennel?" Emmi asked.

It was late in the afternoon, and I knew we had little daylight left.

"Let's take the top of the kennel off and try to coax him onto the blanket with some canned food," I told her. "While he is eating and distracted, we can grab the corners of the blanket and lift him into the kennel."

"We will have to move fast so he doesn't have time to bite one of us," Emmi answered.

I took the kennel top off while Emmi opened a can of dog food, placing small portions close enough for the dog to smell them. He eagerly extended his neck to eat while she kept offering him small pieces of food, encouraging him to come closer to the blanket.

Gradually, he dragged himself forward until he was lying on top of it. Emmi bent down, dumping a larger amount of food in front of him, and while he ate, we quickly picked up the corners of the blanket and lowered him inside the kennel. Placing the top of the kennel back on, we latched the sides.

"What kind of dog do you think he is?" Emmi asked.

"He's missing so much hair, I'm not sure," I said, fastening the last latch. "Maybe an Airedale."

She bent over, looking in. "It is hard to tell. Poor thing."

We picked up the kennel and walked to the van, sliding it inside.

"Do you think someone abandoned him out here?" Emmi asked.

"Well, if he was," I said angrily, "it was the cruelest thing someone could do to him."

Emmi blew on her icy hands, trying to bring some warmth back into them.

"How could someone drive away and leave him out here by himself?" she said, angrily.

"I don't know, but how else could he have gotten out here?" I responded.

We both felt chilled by the thought of it as we looked around the remote, cold woods surrounding us.

"Maybe somehow he got lost," she said, her voice receding into the mist.

The light was fading fast now, so I walked back over to where the dog had been lying and picked the hard hat off the ground. Walking back to the van, I laid it beside the kennel and closed the door. Before climbing into the van, we paused and took one last look around the isolated woods. As we drove slowly down the road, the mist had become thicker, making the trees seem unearthly.

It was cold, and I could feel the desolation and wildness of this place. We drove silently, both in our own solitary thoughts, puzzled by this dog's unfortunate situation. We thought of the uncaring nature of mankind and how they so easily drove away from their dog, leaving him in an unfamiliar place to die. By the time we reached the main road, the sun had gone down completely, leaving no trace of daylight.

I broke the silence in the van. "You know, I don't think he could have lived another night in this cold."

Emmi sighed. "I don't think so either, or some animal might have come along and killed him."

While she drove, I heard her voice quietly say, "I can't stand the thought he may have died out there alone."

"I know," I added. I hope someone didn't intentionally leave him out there.

We drove on in our silent thoughts, downcast.

Turning onto the main road, we drove through a heavy fog until we found a safe place to pull over. Emmi called our director, telling her we had found the dog and the condition he was in.

Hanging up, she looked over at me. "She is calling the closest vet clinic to see if they will stay open to examine him."

Emmi's phone soon rang, and the director told her which vet clinic we were to take the dog to. A half-hour later, we pulled into the clinic parking lot, and a vet assistant hurried out to help us carry the kennel inside.

We told them what we knew about him while placing the kennel on the floor of the examination room. Leaving, we closed the door behind us and sat down in the seating area to wait. A half-hour later, Doctor Clark came out and sat down next to us.

"He's a neutered male around four to five years old," he said.

"He is very weak, severely underweight, and in critical condition. I don't think he would have lived out there in this cold another night, but my primary concern is, I think he may have scabies."

Looking at us closely, he continued, "What you thought was mud caked on him are very large scabs, so I would like to do a skin scrape to be sure."

He sat silently, waiting for us to absorb the information he had given us, and then said, "He is very weak and suffering." He paused. Given the circumstances, my suggestion would be to consider a compassionate euthanasia for him.

"Let me call our director to see what she wants to do," Emmi told him.

Picking up her phone, she stepped outdoors to place the call, and when she returned, she told the vet, "Our director would like you to do the skin scrape."

Placing her phone into her back pocket, she continued, "Once we take possession of an animal, we legally have to hold them for seventy-two hours and try to find the owner. We will take him back to the shelter tonight," she stated determinedly.

Blowing out his cheeks, Doctor Clark nodded. "Okay, make sure you isolate him and don't expose other animals to him. If it is scabies, it is very contagious and can spread to other animals and humans. I will do a skin scrape tonight and call your director tomorrow with the results, but before you go, I would like to start an IV to get some fluids into him."

When we were ready to leave, Doctor Clark patted us sympathetically on the shoulders and then helped us load the kennel into the van. Driving away, the outside temperature had dropped more, leaving the parking lot with a sheen of ice. It was now seven-thirty in the evening.

Icy rain was falling when we arrived at the shelter. The director, along with some of the staff, was waiting for us and had prepared a cozy place in the old building for the dog, away from other animals. We moved him into a warm room, setting the kennel on the floor, and took the top off.

I moved his water bowl close to him and gave him a small amount of wet food. Looking through the kennel bars Pat shared with us she had carefully checked the lost dog log, going back at least six months, but there were no listings for a missing dog in the location where he was found. I picked up the scanner to scan him for a microchip but did not find one. His hairless tail thumped on the side of the kennel.

"Wow, he seems to be a little friendlier now," Emmi said, smiling.

"He knows we are trying to help him," I replied.

Our director's brown eyes teared up as she shook her head in disbelief.

"He was clearly abandoned out there. I will call Dr. Vincent tonight and see if he can come by in the morning to look at him."

"Meanwhile," she sighed, "it is almost nine o'clock, and we need to go home. This has been a very long day."

Emmi placed a floor heater close to the kennel door while I gently laid a blanket over the dog. Walking out of the kennel area, we left the light on, not wanting him to be left alone in the dark. Closing the door behind us, Emmi and I sprayed ourselves down with a disinfectant and silently hoped he would live through the night. But even if he didn't, we knew he was warm and, most of all, safe. Tonight, he was not alone in the cold, dark, freezing woods, or fearing an attack by another animal.

"How did he survive?" we both wondered in our thoughts.

Stepping outdoors, we reached out to give each other a high-five and a weary hug before leaving to go home.

Dr. Vincent drove out to the shelter first thing in the morning. He had been in contact with the vet from the previous evening, who had confirmed the dog had scabies.

Looking closely at our director, he shook his head. "What do you want to do? He's in pretty terrible shape."

"Can he be helped?" our director asked.

Pulling his glasses down his nose, he looked over them at her. "Well, we always give it our best, don't we?" he stated. "It will take him a long time to recover."

We recognized a determined look on his face as he placed his hands on his hips. He gazed at us intently, inhaling and blowing out his breath.

"Honestly, I can't promise you anything, but if you're willing, we can certainly try."

While Dr. Vincent continued with his examination, we nodded in agreement that we wanted to give it a try.

"A veterinarian took the missing leg off; I can see the scar, which is old."

He ran his hands over the dog, checking for injuries, then looked inside his weepy, swollen ears and checked his teeth. Getting his stethoscope out, he put it up against the dog's ribs that stuck out of his emaciated body to listen to his heart.

Consolingly, he patted the dog on the head. "You're such a good dog. I'm sorry all this has happened to you."

Looking up with sorrow on his face, he said, "He had to have been out there on his own for some time."

Thoughtfully, he continued, "I think it would be best if we could place him in a foster situation. I know a vet tech who might want to take him on."

Looking back down at the dog, he continued, "He is going to need a lot of care, a special diet, and a regiment of shampoos and medications."

Looking at our director, he asked, "Would you consider that?"

Our heads turned in unison, looking at her, waiting for her reply. None of us wanted to see him euthanized if we could give him a fighting chance. We all knew he was a fighter because he had been out there alone trying to survive on his own. We couldn't let him down now.

"Yes," our director said, looking at Emmi and me. "These two had to drive for miles and search in the woods to find a half-crazed, starved dog. Then they had to get him safely into a kennel and find their way back in the dark."

Smiling at us, she continued, "The least we can do is to help him. If he doesn't make it, at least his last days are with humans who are caring and kind to him. I hope with all my heart he will recover."

Smiling at us, she said, "Do you want to try?"

Emmi and I nodded our heads in agreement because, as

forlorn and hopeless as he looked, we were not willing to give up on him.

Dr. Vincent smiled. "Well then, what are you going to name this guy?"

"Clayton," I said.

Emmi nodded in agreement. "We had decided on the long trip back to the shelter we would name him Clayton."

"The man who found him is the true hero," I said. "He could have driven off, leaving him there to die, but he didn't."

Emmi smiled. "Since the man's last name is Clayton, we think it's fitting to name the dog after him."

"Perfect," replied our director. "Which reminds me, I need to call Mr. Clayton and tell him we found the dog, and because of his kindness, he probably saved his life. I'll let him know he is here at the shelter and will hopefully go into foster care to recover."

"Well then," said Dr. Vincent. "I'll call Susan and see if she wants to take Clayton on." Relieved, we stood there looking down at Clayton with hope. Later that morning, Emmi and I lathered him in shampoo, starting the treatment regimen Dr. Vincent had placed him on.

When the seventy-two-hour hold was up, Susan, the vet technician Dr. Vincent had recommended, drove out to the shelter to pick up Clayton. We were all relieved to know he was now in excellent hands with a knowledgeable person who would use her training and experience to get him well. We knew the next few weeks were crucial, but he had proved to be a fighter, so we all waited in anticipation for the transformation of Clayton as he emerged from his emaciated cocoon, a fully recovered dog.

Susan spent months working with Clayton. She kept in close contact with our director, sending pictures of him as he regained his health. When we asked our director about him, she would tell us he was doing great but refused to share the pictures with us. She would sit behind her desk, guarding them like a covert Mata

Hari. With a twinkle in her eye, she waved us away, dismissing our curiosity and ignoring our interest.

Picking up the scattered papers covering the top of her desk, she shuffled and paper-clipped them together, dropping them onto one of her many stacks. Then, once again waving her hand, she shooed us out of her office, telling us we would see him soon. Our director loves secrets, and I think she thought of Clayton's recovery as a gift to us, with a special surprise in the end.

Six months later, Susan's car drove into the shelter with a recovered Clayton. Our director greeted her at the front door, excited for Emmi and me to see him. She sent Pat to our offices to get us.

"Guess who's here?" Pat said excitedly.

"Who?" I asked, looking up from my work.

"Clayton."

"Really?" I said, jumping up.

Emmi and I met in the hallway and followed Pat toward the front desk. I stopped in surprise when I saw the beautiful dog sitting beside Susan. Expecting to see an Airedale, instead, there sat a long-haired, black and brown Australian Shepherd. He had a full, luxurious coat that shimmered in health with a white patch on his chest. His eyes filled with trust, and his mouth was friendly as he panted with amiable good nature.

"That's Clayton?" I said, dropping to my knees in front of him.

"Oh wow! He's so beautiful," Emmi said, also on the floor admiring him. "I can't believe how wonderful and healthy he looks."

"He really does, doesn't he?" Susan said, smiling.

He snuggled close to her while we pet him. "He loves everyone, except he is a little quirky and leery around other dogs," she continued. "I wonder if he had to fight off coyotes while out there in the woods by himself."

"Hello, Clayton. You look amazing," I said, touching his soft, full coat.

Tears ran down Emmi's cheeks as she hugged him. "How beautiful you are. What a wonderful surprise."

"I knew you would want to see him," our director said, beaming with joy at our reactions.

"Oh Susan, you have done such a great job with him," I said. "We have been waiting for this day and are so happy to see him."

She smiled back at us. "It was a battle at first, but like you all said, he is a fighter and has a strong will to live."

Clayton bathed our faces with friendly kisses as we pet him, giving him our long-awaited attention. Susan reached down, running her hand through his heavy scruff while speaking with our director.

"I will keep him until you find a home for him."

Disciplining her emotions, she continued, "As much as I would love to keep him, I can't, because I need to be free to help other dogs who may need my help."

Our director walked over to hug Susan. "Thank you so much for helping Clayton. Without your help, he may never have recovered."

"Yes," Emmi said. "Without your care, I don't think he would have survived."

Our director informed her we would start searching for a home immediately, and hopefully, we would place him in the next couple of weeks.

Susan nodded. "I know you will find the perfect home for him. He deserves it."

Now that Clayton was well, our director started hunting in earnest for his new home. She came to my office two days later with the news of a placement for him.

"This is a great home," she said, sliding the application over for me to read.

"They are a retired couple who lost their dog six months ago to cancer. After reading about Clayton on our website, they think he would be a wonderful dog for them."

As I read, she continued, "Susan will bring him by to meet them on Saturday, and if everything goes well, they can adopt him and take him home."

Saturday arrived, and the staff eagerly awaited the couple chosen for Clayton. They arrived at the shelter at one o'clock in the afternoon, and our director introduced Jack and Cindy to the staff. I could tell they were a little nervous but excited to meet Clayton. Cindy told me about her dog, who had died six months earlier and the deep loss they felt. She said they had many discussions on whether to get another dog, but when they read about Clayton on our website, they thought he might fill the empty space in their home.

We showed them pictures of Clayton when he first came in and told them of his rescue. Susan arrived a short time later with him, and we introduced them to Jack and Cindy. Taking them into an office, we left so they could get acquainted and spend time together. Susan told them about him, explaining all the things he liked to do, his daily routine, his likes and dislikes, and about his recovery in her home. Calling his name, Jack invited Clayton over so he could pet him.

"You're a nice, friendly dog," he said. "Would you like to come home with us?"

He ran his hand over Clayton's shiny coat while Clayton wiggled around on his one back leg, trying to wag his tail.

"How much of an impediment is it going to be for him without his leg?" Cindy asked.

"Very little," Susan answered. "He is active and loves his walks. He may be a slow walker, but he gets around very well, don't you, Clayton?"she said, reaching down playfully to ruffle his scruff."

Clayton came over to Cindy and sat down in front of her, leaning on her leg. She gently reached down to pet him, stroking away the loss of her previous dog. Her hand slid over his smooth coat, caressing him with the love she had to give. Cindy and Jack made eye contact from across the room, and it became apparent they were falling in love and would take Clayton home.

Upon completing the paperwork, they were ready to leave. Susan hugged Jack and Cindy, wishing them well. She got down on the floor with Clayton, crying happy tears and hugging him with a last farewell. She was certain he was going to a wonderful home where he would receive love, care, and be kept safe.

Jack promised us they would call to keep us informed about how Clayton was doing. As they left, we stood by the door, happy to watch our courageous Clayton limp out the door and enter his new life with two people who would love and cherish him. We all wiped away tears, knowing that after months of recovery, he was ready to go to his new home.

The next time we saw Clayton, he came to the shelter with Jack and Cindy to receive an award. The shelter established an annual award to honor individuals who make extraordinary efforts to rescue animals. We named it the "Clayton Award." The first year, we gave the award to Clayton's namesake, who on a bitter November day left his hard hat filled with warm soup for a starving dog.

Because he could not put the dog into his company truck and take him to a vet, he tried to call the shelter for help. Later in the day, as he drove away, he could not stand the thought of the dog lying there helpless and alone. He knew the abandoned dog probably could not survive another night without help. Turning his truck around, he drove to the shelter, hoping to find someone who might help him. Many people contributed to Clayton's rescue and recovery, but if this man had not felt concern or empathy and had driven away, we couldn't have saved this wonderful dog from a miserable death in the cold woods.

After shaking Mr. Clayton's hand, we handed him the "Clayton Award." Then Emmi and I handed his hard hat back to him, and as we looked into his kind blue eyes, we saw a hero. With their big hearts, heroes see and feel the need to help the helpless. Not only will they help people, but they also advocate for animals in desperate need of rescue. Every person who helped with Clayton's recovery was a hero, but it all began with one man's big heart.

The love of a dog is a pure thing. He gives you a trust which is total, you must not betray it.

MICHEL HOUELLEBECQ

BENNY

On a wet and gloomy day in January, Benny showed up at the shelter looking extremely thin and weak. We were worried we wouldn't be able to save him.

His ribs and hip bones stuck out of his loose, sagging skin from what had once been a beautiful black and white coat, now dull with patches of missing hair. His head hung low, and his body swayed as he tried to stand on feet burned with urine.

With distress and shock, the staff couldn't help but stare at what should have been a magnificent Great Dane. Anger consumed me as I thought about the person who caused this, questioning their humanity.

The authorities took possession of this Dane and twenty-nine other dogs from a person running a puppy mill. All the dogs were in a sorry state; thin, infested with worms, and ill with Giardia due to contaminated water. They were filthy, with matted hair caked in fecal matter and infested with fleas. Many of the dogs suffered from urine burns on their feet, rotten teeth, and untreated old wounds. Of all these dogs, the Dane whom we would name Benny was in the most critical condition.

The woman responsible for the damage kept him confined in

a wire crate, which was so small he could barely stand and turn around with some effort. I'm always amazed at the cruelty of people and have learned there is a difference between people who run puppy mills and hoarders, but the outcome is almost always the same.

Hoarders, whether because of mental illness or a distorted love for animals, believe they are saving them. However, over time, it will inevitably turn into a disaster. The hoarding situation will spiral out of control because of the overwhelming number of animals rescued. Starting with just a few dogs, cats, or any other animal, the population can rapidly grow to twenty, thirty, or even hundreds. Eventually, they find themselves unable to provide care for the many animals they have taken in.

The act of trying to save and support them triggers a domino effect, as they work tirelessly to ensure secure shelter, cleanliness, and adequate nourishment, all while dealing with the financial burdens of food and veterinary care. Ultimately, it leads to financial stress. Additionally, they experience isolation from loved ones and friends who doubt their intentions and mental well-being.

As these pressures increase, they will sell puppies or kittens to cover their bleeding bank accounts and become evasive with loved ones or individuals who ask too many questions. Becoming more and more reclusive, they cannot understand why people can't see the good they are doing, and in the long run, they harm the animals they love.

Puppy mill people, however, are doing it for the money. The animals that are supposed to be in their care are a commodity, a means to an end. They are only interested in making a large sum of money. If they ever had a genuine love for animals, it has become distorted because of their selfish motives. Pet factories operate by confining animals in dirty crates or wire kennels, posing health hazards. They neglect to provide adequate housing, sufficient food, proper vet care, or grooming for the animals in their care, and they will go to great lengths to save money. They are animal abusers, and what they do is criminal.

If you buy a pet from one of these people, you become an active participant in animal abuse and end up supporting their way of life. It endangers animals, enabling this madness and insanity to continue. You may think you are saving a puppy or kitten, but in reality, you encourage puppy mill people to continue. What is the saying? "Money talks," and that's what drives them. If you need proof of how abused these animals are, visit a shelter and look into a kennel where a dog such as this Dane is, or the other twenty-nine dogs next to him.

This dog would have eventually died in a crate too small for him, standing or laying in his urine or feces. To run in the grass, play with a toy, or have a dry bed was something he would never experience. Without sufficient food and clean water, he would have faced starvation. The soothing sound of a loving voice and the gentle touch of a human hand would always be out of his reach.

In the breeder's eyes, he is a dog used for breeding, which is also true for the female, who may have to produce countless litters until she can no longer breed. Then, if someone doesn't dump them somewhere out in the country, they probably euthanize them. While I'm unsure of the exact method, considering the track record of puppy mills, it's likely not a humane practice.

As I watched this Dane in his misery, all he had ever known was the cruelty of the person who was supposed to care for him. We received him at our shelter with no hope, completely unaware of the experience of being a dog. The most heartbreaking part is that he considered this way of life normal and all he had ever known.

Now, if Benny lives, he will have the experience of knowing human kindness, and learn what it is to be a dog. As the staff stood around his kennel watching this pitiful dog, we each committed and promised to show him a better way of life, one of human kindness and gentleness. Our goal was to assist him in his recovery, tending to both his physical and mental well-being.

For the first time, he will feel the gentle touch of human hands and hear the quiet voices of staff and volunteers encouraging him to be well. He can finally rest easy, knowing there will be enough food, water, and shelter.

Dr. Vincent was the first person we called to examine Benny and the other dogs brought in alongside him. As he entered the kennel area, he stood and gazed at him with tears in his eyes. Gently and methodically, he examined him, making notes and instructing us on how to care for him. He arranged a feeding plan that included regular small meals every two hours, devised a schedule for medicated shampoo baths, and prescribed the required medications to aid Benny's recovery. Standing, he rubbed the stubble on his cheek as if deep in thought.

"I realize this may seem overwhelming, but with his young age and your guidance, I am confident we can help him overcome this. The next few days will be crucial."

I loved Dr. Vincent, a man of remarkable dedication. He always went the extra mile to help animals. Demonstrating genuine advocacy for the animal world, he put in immense effort and commitment to ensure they received the medical care they required. In many situations, his medical expertise played a crucial role in bringing healing to our shelter animals who were sick or injured.

While petting Benny, he said, "I would recruit a couple of extra volunteers to help with his care along with the other dogs, so it doesn't become so overwhelming."

As he made his rounds assessing the remaining dogs, he looked at us with sorrow. "The condition these poor animals are in is truly unbelievable, and it's even more troubling to think these awful places are allowed to stay open."

Giving us a comforting pat on the shoulders, he assured us, "I'll be back tomorrow to see how they're doing."

Benny's recovery started with dedicated staff and volunteers, who showered him with care and encouragement to bring him back to health. We kept a close eye on him, just like protective parents. Every morning when we arrived, our first question would be, "How is Benny doing today?"

He not only had the full attention of his new guardian but also the constant care and protection of Dr. Vincent, who couldn't bear to be away. If he couldn't make it to the shelter, he would call. Benny gradually put on weight, his hair grew thicker, and his tail wagged as he eagerly awaited the arrival of the morning staff.

As the weeks went by, we put Benny in one of the front offices where he could lie on a bed during the day. People who walked by would often stop and ask us about the big dog in the office, wondering if something was wrong with him. We looked at them in surprise because what we were seeing of Benny was so much better than in the previous months. At those moments, we knew we still had a long way to go.

Each day from the office window, we watched Benny starting to show more interest in the world around him. He had never had the freedom to investigate anything, but in the office, he made many new discoveries. Benny used his sense of smell to savor all the wonderful aromas surrounding him and gather information about this new world he could explore. Standing at the window, he looked out, trying to understand what he was seeing for the first time.

Since he still could not comprehend that this place was real, we led him outside, where he enjoyed rolling in the grass and lounging in the sun. He looked at us with amazement, as if to say, "Is this for real?"

With his freedom to roam around the office, his nose led him to the garbage can with its tempting smells, and if there were any remains of food in it, he would joyfully clean it up like a janitor dumping garbage. If staff got distracted for a moment leaving their lunch behind, he happily consumed it.

In his mind, all these delicious-smelling food items were like a great commodity, and free for the taking. He enjoyed being in 'his' office, watching over us while we worked, and sometimes resting his head on our shoulders. If we were not in the room with him, he would rest his head on the desktop, following us with his eyes as we walked by.

We all laughed when Pat said, "Maybe his head feels heavy."

One day, he discovered the half door which led out into the hallway. This provided a great opportunity for him as he could comfortably rest his head on it, observing all the activity in the hall or at the front counter. This drew a lot of attention from the public as they passed by. They asked if they could give him a treat, which gave me the idea of letting them be a part of his recovery.

Giving him healthy snacks contributed to his successful weight gain. Every morning, we placed a specific amount of treats in a small bucket near the door. By doing this, people could give him a treat as they walked past. Benny, stationed by the half door, eagerly kept an eye out for anyone who might offer him treats, his drool trickling down the outside of the door and forming puddles on the floor.

I knew it was teaching him to beg, but so what? There is always an exception to the rule, and Benny was the exception. He became a skilled beggar, pleading with the public until we had to put up signs on the door, limiting him to one treat at a time. This was to prevent all the treats from disappearing before noon and to let him enjoy them throughout the day.

Benny made all kinds of discoveries in the office. I walked around the corner one day to see him trying to position his massive body in an office armchair. It was astonishing to witness the way he contorted his big hulk into a multitude of arrangements. First, he sat like a normal person, his butt pushed back on the seat, and his front feet flat on the floor as he looked around. To become more comfortable, he stood, rotated, and rested his front legs on the chair seat and attempted to adjust his hindquarters and back legs. When that didn't work, he stepped down and jumped into the chair, standing on tiptoe like a child. He tried to lie down by spinning around in circles. With a disappointed sigh, he sat down and positioned himself by placing his right hind leg on the chair and his right front leg on the armrest, leaving his left leg hanging awkwardly. He sat for a moment before standing and moving back to his original sitting position, with his backside on the chair and his front legs on the ground. From the front desk, we watched with amusement as Emmi named it "Benny's Quest of the Chair."

He spent most of the afternoon trying to conquer the chair but finally gave up and took ownership of it by taking a nap with his head under it, snoring loudly. The chair became Benny's. He pushed it around like a child with a toy. He'd put his front paws on it to check out the pictures on the wall or stand on it to get a better view of what was going on in the hallway. Curious about what was happening outside, he even moved it to the window. Any person who dared to sit in it was in for trouble, as he took complete ownership of the chair. If they did, Benny would try to nudge them out, and if that didn't work, he would try to maneuver his great hulk up onto their lap.

We had a volunteer who had grown especially fond of Benny, committing long hours to his recovery. It was through her nursing hands, along with ours, that Benny came back to life. She would show up nearly every day to lend a hand with the extra feedings, wash him with medicated shampoos, and take him outside for his first taste of running and playing.

I could see Benny had fallen in love with her. He knew her voice, footsteps, and smell, and on the days she did not come in, he laid on his bed, his head down, his brows furrowed with a worried look on his face. When she came into the shelter, he would jump on the half door looking out with his deep bark, letting her know he was in the office. This worked well for him because he got an immediate reward when she ran to him, giving him the attention he wanted. When he saw her, he became over-joyed and zoomed around the room in a comically awkward manner. They had bonded, and the staff waited for the time when she would broach the question of adopting him.

After three months in our care, Benny had recovered. He was now at a good weight. His hair had filled in with a thick, healthy shine to his black and white harlequin colors. His eyes were no longer downcast and dull or afraid of the world around him. Instead, he looked with anticipation and confidence, trusting people. He transformed into a beautiful Great Dane, a royal and regal dog.

We knew it was time to let him find a forever home. The volunteer, who had put in so much effort to help Benny heal, approached us with a request to adopt him. Our director and the staff cheered, telling her we were worried she would never ask. We were all very excited and a little sad because he would leave us, but we knew this was the best outcome for both Benny and the volunteer, who had been so loyal to him. He would never lack love, attention, or care, and we would hear from her how he was doing, as she promised to bring him to the shelter to visit us.

The morning came for his adoption, and she came in early after spending an evening in preparation to bring Benny home. With happy tears, the staff arranged for him to leave. With pride and satisfaction, we witnessed a recovered dog who would live out his life in a wonderful, loving home. We all gathered around to give him final pets, kissing him, and not caring how much he drooled on us. We gave her his special blankets, toys, and a giant bed someone had donated for him.

Then, hugging this special volunteer who had worked so hard, we gathered outside the shelter to celebrate, watching as she loaded Benny into her car. She moved around to the driver's side to get in when we heard Pat yelling, "Wait, you forgot something." Turning, she ran back into the building. When she returned, she was carrying Benny's chair. "Of course, the chair!" we exclaimed.

With joy in our hearts, we helped her pack his special chair into the car. Waving, we watched Benny leave with his loyal friend and his chair.

"If a man inspires towards a righteous life, his first act of abstinence is from the injury to animal."

ALBERT EINSTEIN

DOC

Driving into town one morning, I watched a Min Pin high-stepping in front of a baby carriage, pushed by a homeless man. The man had a tall and lean build. His pants were dirty and too short, displaying his bare ankles and mismatched shoes. He talked loudly to his little dog as the dog proudly pranced in front of the carriage like a high-stepping steed. The dog appeared to be healthy, with a shiny black coat and brown highlights over each eye. He seemed happy and content to be on a new morning adventure as he led the way.

Later, when I was leaving town, I once again noticed the pair, this time sitting on a street corner. The man was holding a sign that read, "Could you spare a dollar for my dog and me?" I reached out the car window with some money, but before I could ask him about his dog, the traffic behind me forced me to move on.

The next time I noticed the duo, it was on a rainy day. The same man crossed the street in front of me, still pushing the baby stroller. A large black garbage bag, which flapped wildly in the wind, covered his head and shoulders. A sudden gust of wind blew the sack away and revealed that he was dressed the same as before. His ankles were still bare as he sloshed through the puddles. This time, instead of walking in front of the stroller, the little dog was riding inside, with the plastic sides zipped up tight to prevent him from getting wet. No longer the proud, prancing steed, he was now the prince, carefully wrapped in blankets as he kept watch from his post inside. The man muttered his way through the puddles across the street, waving at each car. As the rain ran down his face, he smiled, pointing to the inside of the stroller, happy to show off his passenger. As I watched him cross on the wet pavement, I was impressed at how carefully this man was taking care of his pet. Even though he was homeless, he was providing a safe haven for his little dog.

As the pair wandered over the city streets, we got calls at the shelter from the public, who were concerned for the little dog's welfare. People called to complain, expressing concern that the dog was neglected and shouldn't be living on the streets. We were receiving so many calls we referred them to the local animal control officer. Soon, she reached out to us to let us know she was aware of the man and his dog, named Doc. She had talked with the police about the man, and they told her there were no records of crime or drug abuse with him. They had one incident where EMTs had been called because he had fallen in the street and needed help to get up. She was told he had a mental illness but was harmless. He had family in the area, but he would not live with any of them. Concerned, his brother bought him the dog, thinking it would help with his mental health issues. She told us to tell the public that both animal control and the police were aware of them, and everything was fine. The calls continued to come in, and we would relay the information to them. Although our response was well-received by most of the public, we received calls from a few pious individuals who expressed their doubts and displeasure.

One Saturday morning, we got a call from a vet tech from a local veterinary clinic. She said they had a Min Pin there, brought in by a woman who claimed she had found it and thought a car had hit him. After examining the dog and doing X-rays, they could not find any injuries. They scanned the dog for a microchip but did not find one. Now they were calling the shelter to see if we had received a missing report on a Min Pin. We searched through the lost dog book but did not find any. We took all their information and then told them to call the police department to see if they had received a report. The clinic called us back later to tell us the police had not received a report on a missing Min Pin, and since the animal control officer was off for the weekend, the dog was to come to the shelter. The vet tech asked us if we could send someone over soon and told us the woman who had brought the dog in was being very persistent in wanting to take him home with her. We told them we would send Pat to pick up the dog and not to release the dog to the woman.

When Pat arrived back at the shelter with him, we all looked into the carrier to see a very feisty Min Pin. Pat took him to the small dog area to set him up in a kennel with a nice, warm bed. He was still barking and growling when I came in to see him. He ran to his bed and burrowed beneath the blankets to hide.

"I hope his owner comes in soon," Pat stated. "He's not thrilled to be here."

I called to him, trying to get him to come out, but he looked at us from under the blanket, growling.

"Does he look familiar?" I said to Pat.

"He looks like a Min Pin to me; they all look alike," she answered back.

I stood thoughtfully watching him, and then it came to me.

"You don't suppose he belongs to the homeless man in town?"

"You mean the man everyone has been calling and complaining about?" Pat said. "How would we ever find him?" She threw up her hands in frustration.

"I don't know," I responded. "Hopefully, Officer Bailey will know where to find him."

I watched the little dog as he poked his head out, still growling.

"If it is the homeless man's dog, this is likely the first time he has ever been away from his owner or kenneled. I wish we could find a baby carriage for him; he might be happier."

Pat laughed. "Well, maybe he belongs to someone else, and they will be in for him soon."

"I hope so," I said, still watching him.

It was the end of the day, and we turned off the lights for the night. I looked back at the little dog on his bed, trying to hide, looking confused and sad.

First thing in the morning the next day, Emmi took a call from a woman asking about the Min Pin at the shelter. As the woman talked, Emmi became suspicious because we had not posted the dog on the website, and she seemed to know a lot about him.

"How did you find out about a Min Pin being brought to the shelter yesterday?" she asked.

"Oh," the woman answered in a syrupy-sweet voice, "because I was the one who found him and took him to the vet clinic." She continued, "The vet tech told me he had to go to the shelter since he was a stray, so I am calling to tell you I am interested in adopting him and want to be the first one in line for him."

Emmi reached for a piece of paper to write on.

"Oh good," she said. "But before I can give you any information about him, I will need your name and phone number."

While Emmi wrote, the woman happily shared her name, address, and phone number.

"Where did you find the dog?" Emmi quizzed her.

"Downtown," the woman told her.

"Well," Emmi said, "I need to let you know we will hold the

dog for seventy-two hours before he will become available for adoption. Hopefully, the owners will come in for him during that time."

"Well, I'm positive they won't," the woman said confidently.

"Why is that?" Emmi asked her.

She stated smugly she believed the homeless man had stolen the dog. "I have seen that poor little thing with him all over town, and I have called animal control many times, but they refuse to help him."

There was a pause on the line for a moment, and then she continued.

"I don't understand why animal control won't help that poor dog. They are letting someone like him to traipse around with a stolen dog. The poor little thing needs a better home than living outdoors on the streets."

"Well, thank you for your call," Emmi said, smiling. "We will be in contact with you as soon as the seventy-two hours are up."

"Thank you, sweetie," the woman said. "You have been so nice."

Emmi hung up the phone, turned excitedly, and gave a thumbs up.

"It's Doc," she said. "Now, how do we find his owner?"

We contacted animal control and told her we had Doc at the shelter, and could she try to find his owner? She told us she would be on the lookout for him and also contacted the police and his family, but it was three days before we heard from her. After searching all over town, Officer Bailey finally located Doc's owner.

"I found him under the bridge, rolled up in a blanket, despondent and crying because he had lost his dog," she said. "Poor man."

"I also made a call to the woman who stole the dog, threatening her with theft. She calls me all the time, and no matter what I tell her, she complains. I'm so sick of her, the piece of (@$**)."

Officer Bailey's colorful language did not surprise us, and on this day and situation, it did not catch us unaware of how she would feel. Officer Bailey had been a drill sergeant in the army, and when she retired, she became one of our local animal control officers. While dealing with many unpleasant situations, she showed great compassion when necessary or asserted her authority by issuing warnings, fines, or confiscating animals in need of her help. She had a tough countenance, and I often wondered if she had many friends, but she loved animals, and their well-being was foremost on her mind. She took her job seriously, and if you didn't respect her, you soon learned to, and it might be the hard way.

"Donald," she smiled, "will be in with his social worker tomorrow to pick up Doc."

She slapped some papers around on the counter.

"Try to talk him into getting Doc micro-chipped," was the last thing she said while walking out the door.

At ten the next day, Donald and his social worker arrived at the shelter to pick up Doc. Donald was agitated and distraught, pacing back and forth, wringing his hands, and talking to himself. Coming to the front counter, he leaned over it and said,

"I'm a good dog owner, yes, I am," rubbing his hand over his eyes and forehead, trying to wipe away the worry.

"Yes, we believe you are," our director reassured him. "Doc is in wonderful condition, which tells me you are a good dog owner, and he has had great care."

"Yes, I take good care of Doc," he stated loudly. "Can I get him back now?"

"Yes, but you need to do some paperwork first, and we want to talk to you about micro-chipping him, so this never happens again."

Donald shook his head no and acted more distressed.

"No, no," he said, pacing again. "I don't want the government tracing me."

Our director watched him as the social worker tried to calm him down.

"Donald," she said, "the government will not be tracing you, but if Doc gets lost or stolen, we will know who he belongs to, and we will get him back to you sooner."

Donald had sat down and was now rocking. Our director quietly talked with him, and we could see him starting to listen to her.

"Doc has missed you very much, and we don't want something like this to happen to him again," our director tried to comfort him. "We will register you as his owner and officially document him at the shelter. The registration will be in your name, and it will be easier for us to know who he belongs to. Then we can notify Officer Bailey, and she will bring him to you."

"Yes," Donald said, now grinning his toothless grin. "She is a nice lady."

Leaning close to our director, he whispered,

"But she has a bad, bad mouth."

"Yes," our director laughed. "She has a very hard job."

"Will it hurt him to be micro-chipped?" Donald asked.

"Only for a moment," she patted him on the hand. "Then we will return him to you, and he will be back in your arms."

"Okay," Donald said, once again rocking.

Emmi and I went to get Doc and micro-chipped him. Then we took him to the office where Donald sat waiting. When we opened the door, Donald looked up to see Doc. He reached out for him, saying Doc's name. Doc squealed with delight, jumping from my arms into Donald's lap. Big tears rolled down Donald's cheeks as he kissed and hugged his dog. Doc licked the tears away, wiggling and squirming, thrilled to be back in his owner's arms. We were happy for them as we watched their joyful reunion and the love this man had for his dog.

"I love you, Doc," Donald said, kissing and petting him.

He looked up at us and smiled, "Thank you, you're nice ladies."

Hugging Doc tight, he said to him, "This is the good life, isn't it, Doc?"

Donald is a person in our society facing mental illness, and has benefited from having companionship from a dog who simply loves him back. Many shelters have started programs adopting dogs to people who are borderline and not living what we would call a normal life. Researchers have discovered that having a dog brings a lot of stability to people who are marginal and need someone to care for or someone to live for. Dogs are great companions who live to love. They love their owners with no prejudice or bias. Along with these programs come free food, leashes, collars, and some veterinarian care. It is not in every community, but in the cities that have started this program, it is successful and supported by donations made by concerned citizens.

Donald and Doc left together that day, and I would see them walking the streets. Donald still pushing Doc in the baby stroller, while waving to people who passed him in their cars. During the winter, Donald and Doc would disappear, and I would not see them again until early spring. Then one warm day, I would once again see them on our city streets. One day in June, I noticed Donald holding up the familiar sign, begging along a busy intersection. Doc sat proudly on the roof of the stroller, looking around and enjoying the warm sun. I got out some money so when I returned, I could give it to him and ask how they were doing. Sometime later, I was driving back toward them, and I could see Donald swinging something in his hand, and he seemed to be in an altercation with two men. Driving closer, I could see he was in a swordsman's stance, his mismatched shoes pointed forward, his knees bent, waving the closed umbrella like a sword, trying to drive his enemies away. Doc was also in the fighting stance as he stood on top of the stroller roof, fearlessly defending his carriage and his person. Legs splayed, and teeth flashing, he was ready to engage in the brawl. Gallant warriors, they stood courageous and undaunted by the two men. I pulled up to the curb and yelled, trying to get the attention of the two men, showing them my phone, hoping they would think I had called the police. They turned to run off, while Donald chased them away, waving his weapon at them.

"Hi, Donald," I said, handing him the money. "How are you and Doc doing?"

"Hello, nice shelter lady," he pocketed the money and picked up Doc to wave his paw at me. "We are living the good life," he smiled his toothless grin. "Doc, say thank you to your friend."

The light turned green, so I smiled and waved back as I drove away. I looked in my rearview mirror while he still held his little dog, waving his paw at me. I watched him as long as I could until they were out of sight, wondering what would happen to them. I couldn't help but think about the last words he said to me, how he believed he was living the good life, and for him, perhaps it was true. Rather than having a home, he found contentment in the streets, accompanied by his loyal little friend.

As the months went by, and it was getting close to fall, I would see Donald pushing Doc in the stroller, happily waving. Then they disappeared again, vanishing into the homeless world. I watched for him the next spring, but never saw him again. When I asked Officer Bailey if she had seen them, she shook her head no. I hoped they had found a quieter place to live, maybe in the woods. Where he could live without people bothering him, thinking he should live like everyone else or not have a dog because they thought he couldn't take care of it. Or maybe he found a safer place, escaping from the criminal element, who tried to steal his begged-for dollars, thinking him an easy target.

Except for his little dog, he was alone in the world. My wish and hope for them is that they are living contentedly together somewhere safe. I still watch for them, and someday I may spot Donald pushing his baby stroller, with Doc high-stepping in front, leading the way, or happily riding inside, as Donald waves.

"No matter how little money and few possessions you own, having a dog makes you rich."

LOUIS SABIN.

FALLON

If there ever was a dog who was a nervous wreck at the shelter, it was Fallon. He was a Greyhound-Labrador mix, tall and slim in stature, with long limbs for running. His coat was black with brown highlights visible in the sunlight, and on the front of his deep chest was a small white patch. When he looked at you with his black liquid eyes, they would catch your attention and capture your soul. I could tell by watching him he had a deep love and trust for people, wanting to be with them. He also had the Greyhound's needy nature, which is part of their charm. As I got to know Fallon, I discovered his anxiety at being left alone led to strange eccentric behaviors.

The first morning I walked into his kennel, he wiggled with anticipation, ready to go outdoors. Grabbing a leash, I went for a walk with him while he contentedly explored the shelter grounds. Coming back indoors, we walked down the hall towards the dog runs, but when he realized he was about to be put back into the kennel, he stopped midway and firmly planted his feet, refusing to go.

"Come on, Fallon," I said, pulling on the leash. "You've had a good outing; it is time to go back."

Like a defiant, willful child, he deliberately laid down on the floor. As I continued to coax him to get up, he stretched out full length, nervously watching me, ready for the challenge. He had no intention of going back to the dog runs, and no amount of coaxing with treats or commands was going to make him move. He stubbornly refused to stand up. I knew I had to win this skirmish, so, putting a sheet under his hind legs, I had a staff member lift as I tried to pull, but he laid there enjoying all the attention. We finally rolled him onto the sheet to drag him back to his kennel.

"I hope he doesn't do this every time someone takes him out," Emmi said, dusting off her hands.

"Me too," I replied, uneasily.

Fallon stood up and sadly watched us as we left. When the door closed behind us, we could hear him howl, and he howled loudly for the rest of the morning. Feeling guilty, I went to check on him early in the afternoon to find his kennel empty. A volunteer was bringing another dog through the dog runs, and I stopped her.

"Has someone taken Fallon out?" I asked.

"No," she laughed, pointing up. "I was just coming to tell you he is up on the ledge."

Looking up, I saw Fallon sitting six feet up on the seven-inch ledge surrounding the inside of his kennel.

"How did he get up there?" I said, looking at him in amazement.

"I don't know, but he has been sitting there since I came in," she laughed.

"Come on, Fallon, get down," I said, pointing to the floor.

He sat there stubbornly, looking down at me, like a sentry on a post. I called Emmi on the radio, and soon all the staff had collected around the kennel, looking up at Fallon.

"What a weird dog!" Pat retorted. "Have you ever seen a dog up there before?"

Emmi and I stood there looking up, shaking our heads no, while Fallon sat there like an Egyptian sphinx, gazing down on us.

Emmi gazed up at him, wondering, "Maybe he doesn't know how to get down."

We thought she might be right, so Pat ran to get a folding table, and we helped her position it under him. He sat there looking down at us while we called to him, trying to coax him to jump down. Finally, he easily jumped onto the table and then to the floor.

"Well, I doubt he will try that again," Pat said.

We moved the table back out, glad we had solved the ledge problem, but an hour later, we had a visitor come to the front desk to inform us a dog was sitting on the ledge in his kennel.

"We know," Pat responded in a casual voice. "He likes it up there."

A few days later, as our director walked through the dog runs, we heard her calling over the intercom.

"We have a dog who is sitting on the ledge of his kennel in Pod A. Could someone come and get him down?"

We went to find her, explaining we could not keep Fallon off the ledge, and he had been sitting there during the day.

"Well, we can't have that!" she informed us. "He may hurt himself, and what will the public think when they walk through and see a dog sitting up there?"

The adventure to outwit this neurotic dog who hated being by himself in a kennel began. To keep him company, we first put another dog in his kennel, but an hour later, they called me in to see Fallon sitting on the ledge while the other dog sat below him, looking up. The next plan of action was to put Fallon in an office during the day, but we soon discovered he had a clever way of opening doors, and we would find him wandering the halls looking for people. We tied the door shut, which worked well, but then he sat and howled forlornly until someone came to retrieve him. Our director thought he would be safer in an office at night as long as he could not get out. Feeling confident, we thought it was worth a try.

On the first night when we left him, he had a nice bed to sleep on, a fresh bowl of water, and toys to play with. Giving him a goodnight pat, we tied the door shut and left. Around 9:00, Emmi was called by our director, asking if she could meet the police at the shelter because the alarms were going off. When she got there, the police were standing outside the front door, looking in at Fallon, who was joyfully wagging his tail at them.

"He's not even a good watchdog," Emmi told me the next morning.

"Where is he now?" I asked.

"In his kennel, sitting on the ledge."

"Maybe we should leave the table in there; he could sit on that," I suggested.

"Nope, we tried that last weekend; he was still on the ledge."

The next round of action we tried was to leave him in the office at night and not set the alarms. The next morning, he was laying outside of the building by the front door waiting for us to arrive. During the night, he had popped the back door open, jumped the fence, and ended up curled in a tight ball by the door. Our director was actively searching for a home for him, but people were not showing any interest. They wanted a dog who they could leave alone if they had to go somewhere.

Out of desperation, we decided a staff member would take him home at night. That way, we would not have to worry about him setting off alarms or running the grounds at the shelter after dark. We were worried he would run out onto the road because the shelter property wasn't fully fenced. Emmi was the first to take him home and reported the next morning all had gone well. Then our director took him home for an evening, but when they left him alone for a few hours, he tore up the blinds in her living room, trying to find a way out. When she brought him back to the shelter the next morning, she looked at us and said, "This dog needs Jesus."

We all laughed at the thought, and later in the afternoon, we drew straws, with Fallon falling into my care for the night. I'm not sure why, but after that, he was always getting into my car to journey home with me each evening. My older dog loved him because he was not too playful and just wanted the companionship of hanging out. He still showed neurotic behaviors if my husband and I left him in the house for a few minutes. He would sit by the door and howl or run from window to window, trying to see where we were.

"How are you ever going to get him adopted?" my husband asked.

"I'm not sure," I replied, concerned.

One evening, we let the dogs out to do their nightly routines before bedding down. Jazz came when we called, but Fallon was not with her. We called with no response, so, grabbing flashlights, we walked around the property to their usual hangouts. We could not hear or see anything of Fallon, and now I was getting worried. I wondered where he could have gone. He never wandered too far from people and would beat Jazzy back to the front door when we called. I walked deeper into the woods, shining the flashlight beam around the trees, but could not hear or see anything of him. Suddenly, I heard my husband's voice calling to me from the house.

"I found him!" he yelled. "He's here in the garage."

I ran back to the house and could see my husband standing by the garage side door. As I walked in, he pointed towards the car. I looked inside, and there was Fallon curled up in a ball, sleeping.

"I must have left the car door open when I came home this evening," he said.

"Well, this is the first time I have seen Fallon so relaxed," I said, looking in at him. "Come on, Fallon, let's go inside."

Fallon lifted his head, looking at me, and then laid it back down, pushing his nose into his curled-up body.

My husband looked over at me. "Let's leave him alone for the night and see what happens. I'll roll the window down so he can jump out if he wants to during the night. I'm sure he will let us know if he wants in."

"I don't know," I said apprehensively. "He will probably wake us up in the middle of the night."

"Well, if he does, we'll let him in."

When we woke the next morning, our first thoughts were on Fallon, who had not made a peep all night. Throwing back the covers, we ran to the garage. When we opened the door, there sat Fallon, looking out the car window at us, fully rested and ready for breakfast. Later, when we sat drinking coffee, we discussed the events of the previous night.

"Maybe he prefers an enclosed place. You could put a big dog kennel on a table in his kennel and see if that works for him," Mark suggested.

"Or buy him a car," I said, laughing.

"Well, whatever you do, I think last night was the first good night's sleep he's had in a month. Look how relaxed he is," he said, pointing at Fallon.

I looked over at Fallon while he lay on a rug, happily chewing on a toy.

"Maybe he was right," I thought. "A kennel on a table might be worth a try."

Arriving at work that morning, I put Fallon in the office and tied the door shut. As I related the previous night's events to the staff, Fallon once again started his howling ritual.

While he bellowed out his howls, I yelled, "Fallon loves cars and slept all night in our car in the garage. He didn't howl one time even though we were not with him."

"Hey!" Pat exclaimed loudly. "We can put him in the old car in the parking lot that was donated to us. It is winter, so he won't get hurt in there, and he can't hurt the old thing because it is already a wreck."

Emmi added enthusiastically, "That way, we won't have to listen to him howl all day. We could go out every once in a while to walk him and let him go to the bathroom."

"Oh, for heaven's sake!" Pat said as she walked to the office door to let him out. "It's worth a try."

"I don't know," I said, happy the racket had ended. "I'm concerned about what our director will think."

"Well, I'm not," retorted Pat defiantly. "It would be a relief to have a quiet day for once."

At that moment, we all came to a silent consensus and ran out to the car, putting in a nice bed, some chew toys, and a water bowl. I got Fallon, bringing him out to the car. He happily jumped in, settling down on his blanket to chew on his toys.

"Perfect," Pat exclaimed. "Look how happy he is."

"Good boy," Emmi cooed. "Have a good day in your car."

Smiling at us, she said, "I'll do first watch and take him out in about an hour."

We spent a quiet day inside the shelter, enjoying the silence. When we went out to check on Fallon, he was happy and tranquil. We took turns walking and playing with him throughout the day. When returning to the car, he happily jumped in, laying down to take a nap. Going home with me in the evenings, he seemed more relaxed and content. Even though he had spent all day in a car at the shelter, when bedtime came, he still wanted to sleep in my car.

His new daytime routine went on for a week, with everyone happy. Then late one afternoon, when our director was returning to the shelter after a long day of meetings, she noticed a dog sitting in the donated car, looking out at her. It is not unusual for people to abandon their pets in the shelter parking lot, so she assumed someone had put a dog in the car. She walked up to the front doors and yelled in.

"There's an abandoned dog in the donated car!" she said, pointing. "We need to get staff out here right now and get him out."

We walked outdoors to see Fallon sitting in the front seat, looking out of the car window.

"Oh," said Pat. "That's not an abandoned dog, that's Fallon. He enjoys being in a car."

Our director stood there for a minute, trying to absorb what she had just heard. She stared at Fallon, who was sitting with his tongue happily hanging out. She turned around with an angry look on her face.

"Get Fallon out of that car!" Her voice rose another octave. "We don't do things like that around here; what are you thinking?"

She turned back around and stormed into the building. We pulled a resistant Fallon out of the car and put him back into the office, where he unhappily howled for the rest of the afternoon. That evening, I took him home, and when bedtime came, he went to the garage door and sat down to wait for me. I opened it, and he walked over to the car to be let in. I could not refuse him this moment of happiness, free of anxiety, so I opened the door and rolled down the window. Fallon jumped in, curled up on his blanket, and giving an enormous sigh, he laid his head down and went to sleep.

The next morning, our director called the staff up front to lecture us on what we should never do at the shelter. Shouting over Fallon's howls, she reminded us, "The public has a certain perception of us, and we are to be the leaders in animal care in our community."

"Yes," she shouted. "I know it is winter, and Fallon would not get hurt in a car, but the idea of it is unsettling, and you are never to do that again."

We all apologized, while Fallon, not happy at being separated from his beloved car or people, continued to cry in protest from the office behind us for the rest of the day. I couldn't wait to get him home that evening so he could have an untroubled sleep in the serenity of my car.

Now that Fallon was confined to an office, he persisted in his wailing howls at being left alone. Our director madly continued to look for a home for him, and finally, exacerbated by all the noise, she would yell from her office, "Would someone please take that poor dog out for a walk?"

We would put a leash on Fallon to go out, but as we walked outdoors, he would try to drag us towards his beloved car. Now, we assigned a staff member to be confined in the office with him to ensure people at the front desk could work peacefully. Sometimes the staff had to leave him alone because they needed to help with other animals. On one particular day, I had to leave to take a sick dog to the vet. When I left, I could hear Fallon waging war with a full belt of combat howls hurled from behind the office door. Later, when I returned to the shelter, I drove into the parking lot to see the window rolled down on the donated car, and there inside sat Fallon, happily looking out at me.

I walked into the building and whispered to Pat, "Someone has put Fallon in the car!"

She averted her eyes down, nodding her head towards the director's office door.

"What! You mean she put Fallon in the car?"

She was shaking her head up and down, confirming what I said was true, when I heard our director's voice.

"Oh, Julie, I put Fallon in the donated car that's sitting in the parking lot." She continued in a singsong voice as if she had just thought of it and what a grand idea it was. "He seemed so unhappy, so I put a nice bed, water, and rolled the windows down. It will be a nice safe place for him, and he loves it out there."

She was quiet for a moment and then continued. "Don't you think that is a great idea?"

I stood there shocked, and before I could respond, she looked around her desk to inquire, "Oh! Would you take him for a walk in about an hour?"

With that statement, she turned back to her computer while I stood there, open-mouthed. She continued to work, not looking up, and then the next request came.

"Could you please shut my door? I have so much work to get done today."

Pat gave me a sideways glance as I threw up my hands and walked over to her door, shutting it, but inside my mind, I had just slammed it.

This car scenario went on for a couple more weeks while staff members desperately tried to resolve Fallon's separation anxiety. We knew we needed to place him in a home, but when we were open about his separation anxiety, people would politely back out, not wanting a dog who couldn't be left alone unless he was in the family car.

One day, as we were discussing the obstacles we were facing with Fallon, a staff member named Heather said, "I wonder if my Auntie would take him."

We all glanced up at her, anticipating what she was going to say next.

"She lives alone and has cancer but seems to do okay."

She looked around at all of us. "She has been talking about getting a dog and has read somewhere that animals can help in recovery."

"Well!" Pat said in her usual skeptical voice. "I don't know if a dog with mental issues is a good idea when someone is trying to recover from cancer."

"Well, you don't know my Auntie!" Heather retorted. "She's a fighter, and if she thinks a dog would help her, the more power to her. Besides," she continued, "this is the first time in her life she has been without a dog. Not only has she had dogs, but she has taken on some difficult dogs in the past."

"Are you sure, Heather?" I said, as my hopes rose.

"All I can do is ask her," she said, shrugging her shoulders. "I'll be completely honest with her; maybe we can do it on a trial basis."

She looked across the table at us. "What have we got to lose?"

Watching Heather closely, I had to ask, "What will happen to Fallon if your Auntie dies?"

"One of her kids will take him. They're all dog nuts. Fallon would fit right in."

Heather had worked at the shelter for five years. She was a hard worker, confident, and had a gift of gab. She loved her family, always telling the staff stories about their holidays together and adventures. I knew if she felt confident about her Auntie and her abilities with dogs, this might be a great fit for Fallon. It was a couple of days before she mentioned anything about her Auntie taking Fallon. We were taking a break outside when she took her cigarette from her mouth, lifting her head to blow smoke into the air.

"My Auntie is interested in Fallon," she said, smiling. "She is coming on Saturday to visit with him."

"What did she say about all Fallon's quirks?" I wanted to know.

"I was very truthful with her, even about the car, but she said that is not a problem."

"Not a problem!" I retorted, looking at her as she blew more smoke over her head.

"She told me she has a doctor's prescription for a service dog and can take him with her wherever she goes, so she thinks it won't be a problem."

Stomping out her cigarette, she said, "I'm talking with the director right now. Do you want to come along?"

"Sure," I said, smiling. "But first, let me get Fallon out of the car and put him in the office."

We sat down to talk with the director about Heather's Auntie while Fallon hurled out his best howls from the office.

"Why isn't Fallon in his car?" she inquired, squinting her eyes as if in pain.

"Because it is a little too warm this afternoon for him to be in there," I replied.

Leaning around her desk, she yelled at Pat, "Pat, please go into the office with Fallon. You can work in there."

Pat grabbed her papers, looking cranky, as she stomped towards the office door. Now it was quieter, and we could talk about Heather's Auntie. Our director asked important questions about her, her living situation, her family support, and most importantly, what would become of Fallon if things went terribly wrong? Heather answered all her questions and then sat quietly, waiting for her response. Our director sat there, thumping her pen on the desktop in thought. Finally, she glanced at us, saying, "Well, this could be the answer we need for poor Fallon. I would adopt him to her on a trial basis, and I hope it will work for both of them. Tell your Auntie to come on Saturday, and if all goes well, we will send Fallon home with her."

Leaving her office, we smiled. Maybe at last, we had found Fallon a home. When we walked into the office where Fallon was, I put his leash on him.

Pat looked at me, saying, "I just took him out; where are you going with him?"

"I'm putting him back in the car," I said.

"I thought you said it was too warm out there," Heather questioned me.

"It has cooled off, hasn't it, Fallon?" I replied, grinning.

"Oh, tricky! Way to go, tampering with the director," Pat laughed.

I smiled while opening the door. "I was just reminding her of the daily concerts and that summer is coming."

On Saturday afternoon, Heather's Auntie came. When she

walked through the doors, she had an entourage of family members, ready to announce to us their mom, sister, and Auntie needed a dog. Heather went to get Fallon out of the car, while we ushered Auntie and her family into an office where she would meet him. Our director stepped in and introduced herself to all of them and asked everyone to step into the hall except Heather's Auntie. While she sat playing and visiting with Fallon, our director talked with the relatives, pelting them with questions on how their loved one would do with a dog who suffers from separation anxiety. They all assured her she had owned many dogs, and some of them had problems which she had coped with very well. As a family, they had been with her every day, helping her to struggle through her cancer and treatments. Auntie's sister told our director she has been talking about getting another dog, and they all felt it was a good time for her to do it. Her son looked at our director and summed up how they felt.

"When mom got cancer, we were devastated, but we soon learned cancer affects the whole family emotionally, even if not physically." If having a dog in her life gives her hope, companionship, and someone to live for, then that is what we want for her. We have talked with each other these past few days about this dog, and it sounds as if he needs my mother as much as she needs him. He will have the best home, with a lot of love, not only from mom but from all of us."

He looked through the window at his mom while she sat on the floor petting Fallon.

"They need each other," he said.

Our director looked over his shoulder.

"Well, you are very eloquent and have made a wonderful case for your mom, but I think you should hear how he howls if no one is with him."

With that, she opened the door, asking Heather's Auntie to step out into the hall. As soon as the door closed, Fallon started his hullabaloo with all of us wincing. But instead of Heather's family being repulsed by all of his fuss, they ran to the door with sympathetic concern. They opened the door so Fallon could come out to be showered with loving reassurances. Our director knew at that moment Fallon had found his home. The family all crammed into the office while Heather adopted Fallon to her Auntie. After completing the adoption, Auntie pulled a red service vest out of a bag she carried. Her son helped her put it on Fallon, making it official he was now in service.

For the next couple of weeks, we heard stories about how Fallon and Auntie were doing, how she had resolved the car issue by letting him sleep with her at night. Heather told us Fallon still loved cars, and he would take a nap in her Auntie's car, but as time went by, that happened less and less. Like all the dogs who get adopted, they blend into their new families' lives, and we don't hear about them.

It had been seven years since Fallon's adoption. Heather left the shelter for another job, and after my retirement, she called one morning, asking if we could meet for lunch. When I asked her how her Auntie and Fallon were doing, she looked at me sadly.

"My Auntie is doing well, but she is sad because Fallon passed away a couple of months ago."

I felt sadness for Heather's Auntie and Fallon's passing, but I also felt happiness knowing this dog, who was so distressed in the shelter, had found a secure, loving home where he was needed and had made such a difference in someone's life. He brought her companionship and love while she coped with the dreadful disease of cancer, and she had brought a calm presence into Fallon's life while he coped with separation anxiety.

Who would have thought at the time she would have outlived her dog? It goes to show when you have someone to love and live for, such as a dog or an animal, it brings joy and gives hope. Well done, Fallon. You did a great thing for a person in need, and well done, Auntie. The loving, secure home you provided gave an anxiety-ridden dog a new lease on life. You are both champions.

"Dog's, are not our whole life, but they make our lives whole."

ROGER A. CARAS

IKE

"I hate him," she yelled as she leaned over the front counter, her mouth open in a scream, waving her arms toward our director. I approached the front counter, noticing a black and white flat-coated Border Collie standing behind the screaming woman. When we hear a disturbance in the building, staff members immediately drop what they are doing to mobilize and go to where the trouble is, in case the police need to be called.

People can be bizarre when it comes to their pets, and we have discovered that some people think they will get their way by being dramatic, bullying us, or even threatening us. This woman was doing all three as she leaned over the front counter, flinging abuses toward our director. Even though our director was trying to be pleasant, she remained firm as she tried to explain the shelter's policy.

"You mentioned," she said, "you took possession of this dog one month ago, so you are considered the legal owner in this state, and you will need to pay the intake fee to bring him in."

"Plus," she added, "we would like you to give us as much information on him as you can. This will help us make an informed decision about finding a new home for him.

Spit flew across the counter as the woman screamed, "I pay my taxes, and I will not pay another cent toward this dog!"

She shook her finger at our director. "When I left him home alone for a couple of hours to go to the store, what does he do? He tears my entire house apart."

Her face was crimson red by now, her voice escalating. "I can't trust him to be left alone, so I put him in the garage, and now he barks all the time," she yelled.

I stood near the phone, watching this difficult woman displaying her wretched behavior as she continued to yell. "He's supposed to be a companion dog, but he never obeys me. He gives me weird looks and stares at me. Now if I yell at him, he shows his teeth. I think he is stupid and dangerous," she said, looking down at the dog and wiping the spit away from her mouth.

"If you don't take him, I will take him out into the woods and dump him."

I looked down at this poor dog and knew that if he could speak in a human voice, he would say, "I hate her too. She is mean and yells, yells, yells all the time."

Our director raised her hands in a resigned gesture, trying to calm the woman down. She could tell there was no way to reason with this mean-spirited woman, so now she was trying to get her out of the building and off the shelter property.

"Okay," she said in a resolved voice. "We will take him, but you need to know we are not government or county-funded. We are a nonprofit organization with all our funding coming from the community, from people who care and love animals."

Trying not to sound exasperated, she continued, "We will not charge you if you will give us as much information on him as you can."

The woman's countenance changed, as she felt satisfied that she had gotten her way. Grabbing the intake form, she filled it out in illegible handwriting. Looking toward the staff, our director motioned for us to get the dog. Meanwhile, the woman continued to complain.

"His owners," she said, grumbling, "told me they had started him on training to herd sheep. They were in the Navy, being deployed overseas, and being the nice person I am, I told them I would take him off their hands."

Waving her hand in the air, she stated, "I even paid them five hundred dollars for him, because he is a purebred."

Our director questioned her, "Have you tried to contact the original owners? Maybe they would take him back."

"No," she said, annoyed. "They moved to Japan and did not leave me a phone number."

"I doubt that," I thought.

I knew she would not give us any further information, but I was glad this poor dog was now in a safe place and hopefully he was micro-chipped so we could contact the original owners. When she turned to leave, she lifted a plastic sack, pulling out a thick manila envelope, and dropping it onto the countertop.

"There may be more information in there," she said. "I have not had time to open it."

I reached down to pick up the dog's leash, asking her, "What is his name?"

"I named him Rocky," she said with a half-smile, brushing me off as she walked away.

When she reached the outside door, she turned with a pleasant smile and, in a sweet voice, said, "You all have a wonderful day."

I don't know if these kinds of people can read our thoughts, or maybe it is better if they don't.

"What a rude, awful person," I sputtered.

In my thoughts, I was calling her far worse names.

Pat truthfully and bluntly declared, "She's an asshole."

Our director rolled her eyes. "Yes, some people are really difficult and hard to love."

I wondered if she really thought that, or if she was having the same wicked thoughts we were having. Sometimes she seemed way too nice.

The taillights flashed on as the woman turned out of the parking lot, and I wondered what Rocky was thinking while he watched the car leave. I fantasized he was also calling her terrible names or at least sticking out his tongue for a last farewell, but I'm sure as far as he was concerned, terrible names were sufficient.

I always wonder why people take on some breeds without reading up on them. The Border Collie is an intelligent, resilient breed and can be quirky as part of their nature. They are very loyal and selective, expecting their daily routines, and dislike their regimen to change. There is a time to wake up, eat, exercise, work, and sleep. Their loyalty is towards one person, and that is their owner. If you take on this breed when they are adults, you will need to give them plenty of time to become acquainted with you because they do not do well in new situations.

I looked down at Rocky as we walked away from the front counter and invited him to go outdoors before settling him into a kennel. I stood watching him smell around the play yard and wondered what he had experienced in the unpleasant woman's home. He looked back at me distrustfully, so I sat down on a bench to wait quietly so he could get his bearings.

As he smelled and walked the perimeter of the fence, he marked over the other dogs' scents, then went to the water bowl to get a drink of water. Finally, he came over to where I was sitting, laying down a short distance away. I didn't try to pet him, but spoke to him in a low, soft voice. I knew he would accept me on his own terms once he felt he could trust me. We sat there twenty minutes before he got up to check the perimeter again. Finally, looking back at me and perceiving I was not a threat, he came over and sat down next to me. I reached out to pet him gently on the head, sympathizing with him and allowing him to be in a calm, quiet place.

"You're a good boy, Rocky," I said. "I will make a promise to you to find a better home for you than the one you just came from. The old hag."

He looked up at me with his brown intelligent eyes.

"You tore her house up on purpose, didn't you?" I said, smiling.

I patted him on top of his head. "It was the least you could do, wasn't it?"

I laughed out loud and couldn't help feeling smug about the mess he must have made.

"Yup, a one-dog demolition crew," I said, laughing more.

He looked back at me as if to say, "You have no idea."

I picked up his leash, clipping it to his collar to take him back inside and find him a nice, quiet kennel for the night.

The next morning, I got Rocky and took him for a mile hike. Tired, we returned to my office so I could evaluate him. He seemed wary of me at first, but soon settled in, showing me a slight uncommitted wave of his tucked tail. I did not blame him for being guarded. I'm sure losing the people he loved and his familiar routine confused him. Then, they sent him into a home with a screaming, impatient woman who clearly disliked him. Now he was in another unfamiliar place, surrounded by noisy, barking dogs.

In my office, he relaxed, smelling around the room. Crawling up on the bed, he circled several times to lie down. Placing his head down on his front paws, he laid there quietly, observing me. I put some dry dog food in a bowl and set it down on the floor in front of him. Working himself forward, he leaned over the bowl to look inside. He got off the bed, walked over to smell the food, and then removed one kibble at a time, placing it meticulously on the floor beside the bowl. After removing all the food, he started eating.

"You're bored," I said, laughing. "Or is this one of your Border fetishes?"

Crunching on his food, he looked up at me like this was the normal way of eating.

"Do you want to go outside to work?" I asked.

His ears pricked forward, showing interest. I leashed him up, and we went out to the play yard. I let him snoop around for a time, and then, calling him over, I raised my closed hand.

"Rocky, sit," I said.

He intently watched my hand and started to sit, but then stopped.

"Rocky, lay down," I commanded, pushing my open hand down in the down position.

His body started to lower, but again, he stopped.

"I thought she said they had started you in herding classes."

I looked down at him while he stared at me with his Border Collie stare. He acted like he recognized and understood the commands, but he would not do them.

"Rocky, away," I shouted.

He started to the right, but again stopped.

Puzzled, I called out, "Come by."

He jumped to the left but again stopped to look back at me with a confused look. By recognizing the commands, I knew he had been trained in herding, but why did he choose to stop? Was it because he was just stubborn, or was it because there was not anything to herd? Was that why he looked at me as if I was some kind of ignoramus and had lost my mind?

We had a barn on the shelter property with chickens, so I took him down to see if he would obey the commands if he had something to herd. When he saw them, he became alert and focused, so I tried the same herding commands I had used earlier with the same results. Puzzled, I brought him back to the main building. I grabbed his paperwork that was still lying on the front counter as we walked by.

In my office, I opened the manila envelope, pulling the papers out and laying them across the top of my desk. On the top of the pile was his vet information, and when I picked it up, a certificate dropped out. Unfolding it, I laid it across my desk and discovered it was an AKC pedigree certificate. It had his registration number, the names of his parents, grandparents, great-grandparents, and great-great-grandparents, with their certifications. Also included was a description of Rocky and his name, which was not Rocky, but a long name, including both his parents. Obviously, they would not call him by his papered name, and had shortened it to Ike.

I looked over at him. "Ike," I said.

His ears pricked forward as he recognized his name, and he looked at me with interest, wagging his tail.

"Okay, my friend, now I know what your real name is," I said.

I reached down to pet his soft ears while I continued to read the certificate in amazement.

"Wow, look at this lineage," I said. "This is impressive. Did you know you were born into royalty and that they are all champions?"

I sat back in my chair contemplating, then grabbing his leash, we hurried down to the barn to herd some chickens. Now, as I used his correct name, he worked in his awkward juvenile way. The chickens clucked and ran as he stalked them, riling them up out of their barnyard lethargy. They flew in every direction— here, there, and beyond—over his head. After working with him for a while, I took him back to my office and leave the unfortunate, badly perturbed chickens alone. I had the information I needed, and we would try to place him in a home where he could herd.

A couple of days after Ike had arrived, one of my friends, Cathy, a fellow dog lover, came into the shelter to walk the dogs.

While making her rounds through the kennels, she noticed Ike and hurried to my office to ask me about him.

"Who's the beautiful dog in kennel 30?" she asked, sitting down.

"That is Ike," I said, as I shuffled through papers, pushing his pedigree papers toward her.

She read it, whistling. "Wow, this is impressive. Where did you get him from?"

I told her the story of how his family had been deployed to Japan. He was sold to a woman who, after he had demolished her house, brought him to the shelter.

"Oh, the Border Collie one-man wrecking crew," she laughed.

"And she deserved it," I added. "She was awful."

Standing up, I asked her, "Would you like to watch him work the chickens?"

"Sure," she said.

I grabbed my leash, and we went to get Ike. We walked him down to the barn to herd the same flustered hens. Ike was immediately interested and went down into the stalking position, looking back at me, ready for a command. We watched him as he walked up on the chickens while they squawked and ran, helter-skelter, around the barnyard.

Smiling, I said, "I have to stop this, or they will quit laying."

Cathy watched Ike move forward toward the chickens.

"This dog needs to work; he needs a home where he can herd," she said.

"I know," I said, smiling.

I gave him the come-by command, and we watched him circle the chickens, laughing as they flew over his head.

"You know," she said, "I have a friend who might be interested in him. She has been talking about getting a working breed for her mini-farm."

"Are there sheep there?" I asked.

"Yes, and a few goats, but I don't think she has ever worked with a herding dog before, but she could take some classes."

"Well, this would be a great dog for her farm," I said, calling Ike over to me.

"Call her and tell her about him because the less time he spends here, the better it will be for him."

"I'll call her tonight and see if she is interested," she said. "I'll let you know."

I knew once the shelter posted Ike on the website, we would receive a lot of applications for him, but if he could go into a home where he could develop his herding skills, it would be the ideal placement for him.

Cathy called me a few days later, asking if she could bring her friend to the shelter to meet Ike. On the afternoon they came, the weather was awful with a heavy rainstorm. The gray of the sky blended with the gray of the asphalt, and a deluge of rain pounded the pavement.

It was still raining when Cathy and her friend came. Soaking wet, they shook the rain off their coats as Cathy introduced Leah to the staff. Leah was a petite woman in her mid-thirties with a quiet demeanor. Her quietness made her seem unsure, and in a soft voice, she told me about her mini-farm with all her beloved animals. While she talked, another side of her personality presented itself. She told me in a very determined voice she would not tolerate a dog who would chase or harm her animals. I could see strength in her then—a toughness and fortitude which could handle a working breed dog.

I sat there watching her, thinking herding classes would be great for both of them. In classes, Ike could develop his natural ability to herd, and Leah would learn leadership skills with a herding breed while gaining confidence as a dog handler. I pushed Ike's paperwork across my desk for her to read, hoping she would understand who Ike was and the champion blood lines he had come from.

While she read, I left the room to get Ike and bring him back to my office for her to meet. When he walked into the room, he noticed the stranger sitting there and immediately sat down beside me to watch her from a safe distance. It was too wet to go outdoors, so we left them alone in my office so they could get acquainted. Leah had filled out an application on Ike, handing it to me when she came in. I rolled it in my hands, hoping this would be a good match.

Cathy and I talked for a while, and then she walked back across the hall to watch Leah and Ike through my office window. When I stepped into the hallway, she turned toward me, smiling, and nodding, gave me a thumbs up. I unrolled the application and walked to my director's office. She asked me a lot of questions about Leah and how I thought Ike would do in her home. After listening to my positive responses, she picked up a red pen, signing her name across the top of the application, approving Ike's adoption.

As she handed it across her desk toward me, she told me, "I'll approve this if she will take him to herding classes."

I ran down the hallway with the approved application, showing it to Cathy.

"What do you think? Will she follow through with herding classes?" I asked.

Cathy looked at me, grinning. "I have known Leah for years, and when she takes on a project, she puts her heart and soul into it."

We both looked into my office window, seeing Leah sitting on the floor playing with Ike.

"They approved her application, but only if she will take him to herding classes."

"Well, let's go in and see what she's thinking," Cathy responded.

Leah was on her phone when we walked in. Getting off the floor, she turned and lifted her phone toward me.

"Have you ever heard of this person?" she asked me.

On her phone was the name of a very respected trainer who had taught herding classes for years.

"Yes," I told her. "He is a well-known, respected handler and teaches classes. I have heard he judges competitions throughout the Northwest."

"Well, I have placed a call to him and scheduled a class for Ike next week, but I wanted to know if you thought this was a good place to take him," she replied.

I stood there smiling, happy she had been so proactive.

"Are you ready to take Ike on?" Cathy asked.

"I would love to," Leah smiled. "It will be an interesting challenge for both of us."

I bent down to pet Ike. "He likes his name and will not listen to you if you try to change it," I told her.

She looked at me, surprised. "Why would I change his name?"

I smiled and stepped out of the room to find a staff member to complete Ike's adoption.

We sent him home on that rainy afternoon. Ike settled into his new home with Leah, and they started their new life together, learning the art of sheep herding. Cathy would tell me how Ike and Leah were doing on the days she came in to walk dogs. One morning, when I entered my office, I found a note on my desk from Cathy. The note mentioned that Ike and Leah had received an invitation to the AKC local herding competition. Ike had received two ribbons for 2nd and 4th place. I smiled, remembering what Cathy had told me about Leah—how she would take on new projects fully committed. A year later, Leah called me to tell me Ike had competed in a big herding trial. He had won the class, taking home first place. I was so proud of him and overjoyed he had found a home where he could do what he loved and was bred to do.

Later in the year, I came to work one morning to see a

framed picture laying on my desk. It was a collage of four pictures of Ike herding sheep in a competition. In two pictures, he was stalking; in another, he was intently staring at the sheep. The one I loved the most was the one of him standing sideways, his head turned toward the camera, looking happy and content. There was a note attached. The note thanked me for Ike and informed me that Ike received an invitation to compete in the Mountain State Stock Dog Association competition. Wow, I thought, smiling as I hugged the picture close to me. He had come full circle. He came from a place where the people he loved had given him up to a woman who did not understand his breed and hated him. She brought him into the shelter where he then went to a home with a woman who was willing to work and train him, bringing out the best in his breed. Together, they learned the skills which gave him a purpose in life as a working dog and helped him to become a champion.

I proudly hung his picture on my wall, feeling such pride and satisfaction to have been a part of this dog's life. He is one of my treasured memories; his picture still hangs in my home. You might also wonder what was the outcome of the Mountain State Stock Dog Association Competition? He took first place with confidence, skill, and mastery. Coming from a long line of champions, he became proficient in what he loves and was trained to do, and he took his place among them. True to his lineage and Border Collie breeding, a champion.

"Once you have had a wonderful dog, a life without one is a life diminished."

DEAN KOONTZ

GIZMO

My job at our local shelter was to evaluate dogs to determine the type of home they needed to succeed. A home where they could be a part of a family, or perhaps an adult-only household. Our goal was to place them where they could flourish, never having to return to a shelter again. Often, it was a matter of getting the dogs neutered or spayed so they could settle their hormonal minds, allowing them to focus on learning good dog manners. With a little training, they would become good canine citizens, making it easier to meld into their future human pack.

Owners often brought their dogs to the shelter in exasperation, complaining the dog was out of control and causing havoc in their home. They would tell us their dog would not listen and list behaviors like dumping the garbage, jumping on children, chewing up furniture, and counter surfing. The final straw was often when the dog chewed up their owner's favorite expensive shoe or the television remote, forcing them to leave their chair each time they wanted to change the channel. Instead of a nice evening walk or playtime, the family banished the dog to the backyard, isolating it from them. Ignored and not allowed to be a part of the pack, they barked excessively, becoming a neighborhood nuisance.

The once cute little puppy had turned into a monster, and the owners had had enough. Out of frustration, they called the shelter, asking if they could bring in their dog. Arriving, they gladly paid the intake fee, handed over the dog's food bowls, toys, and blanket, and walked away without looking back, thinking they had solved their problem.

Through our experiences at the shelter, we have found various factors can lead to a dog's problematic behavior. Through experience, we have found most of these dogs come in around the age of six months to two years old. They are usually not neutered or spayed and have had little training. Without training, exercise, and social interaction, they haven't picked up the skills to handle boundaries or navigate the complicated human world.

Once a cute little puppy, they now have a full-sized dog with the mind of a puppy. Not trained and lacking interaction from their owners, they are a loose cannon, with the family growing tired of them. As we watch the people leave, we know they have learned nothing from their experience, and in a year or less, they will bring another puppy into their home, starting the cycle all over again. Once again, never getting their new dog neutered or spayed, or taking them to training, the dog will not learn a healthy way to become a family member. The owners never learn how to bring out the best in a dog, and sadly, they never become good dog owners.

When we see the bewildered and unpredictable dog in front of us, we are confident once they are spayed or neutered and receive some training, we can find them a suitable family to adopt them. A year later, the new adopters will call us to tell us what a wonderful, calm dog he or she is, and they cannot understand how anyone ever gave them up. We will smile, happy for all of them, especially the dog. Hanging up, we will wait for the original owners of the dog to call, once again frustrated and wanting to bring in their new puppy, now a dog they had to have.

Now, this is not true for every dog, and sometimes a special case comes through the shelter doors, like Gizmo. His owners had brought him in at their wit's end after doing everything right. They had him neutered, gave him puppy classes, which he had flunked out of, and walked him twice a day for an hour each time, but even after a lot of exercise and playtime, they could not control his high energy. They had tried everything they could, with no success in calming him. After several incidents, they felt he needed a more energetic home or a trainer who could put the hours into him they could not and were no longer willing to do. With a sense of sadness and feeling they had failed him, they paid the intake fee and unhappily walked away.

The morning I walked into Gizmo's pod area, I looked into his kennel to see a two-year-old chocolate Labrador mixed with Pitbull. When he saw me, he sat down, his body quivering from the top of his head to the tip of his rapidly moving tail. I could tell this dog was ready for action, and if his body responded like all the pent-up energy making him shake, he might be hard to control. As he sat looking at me, his eyes were intense but friendly. He barked once, waiting to see if I would respond. When I did not, he barked again. I whispered quietly to him, watching for a reaction, as I do for all the excitable dogs, but he stayed in his sitting position.

When I felt he had calmed down enough and would mind his manners, I opened his kennel door and slowly stepped inside. He never moved until I shut the door, and then all hell broke loose. In one giant leap, he sprang at me, happily jumping and zig-zagging around the kennel. Coming back towards me, he was an out-of-control maniac. His wild behavior escalating, he mounted my leg to hump on it. Grabbing him by the collar, I pulled him off and put the loose lead over his head. Once the lead was on him, I could hold him at arm's length, preventing him from coming close to me.

Knowing I was in control of him, he settled and sat down when I told him to. As soon as I thought he was ready to listen, I slowly opened the kennel door. Seeing the open door, he took full advantage of the opportunity by propelling forward, jerking the leash from my hand. Lunging through his kennel gate, he ran to the end of the hall, vaulting with full force at the next door. As he slobbered all over the window, he looked back at me to make sure I was coming. I picked up the leash and waited for him to calm down, telling him to sit. He sat, looking like a perfect gentleman, but I knew this dog had an agenda, and I was a means to an end for him, which was to get out the door. I braced myself for the next excursion into the hallway.

When I opened the door, he shot through, repeating the same antics, only this time I had a good hold on his leash. In the hallway, we flew by the front desk with the staff watching wide-eyed. Gizmo was pulling for all he was worth, running with wild abandon as I tried to keep up. When we reached the outside door, he jumped on it, pushing it open. Once we were in the fenced area, he again jerked the leash from my hand when he spotted a ball lying on the ground. Grabbing it, he ran wildly, shaking his head from side to side, galloping around the play yard.

Watching him, I wondered what he would do next. Would he come over and try to include me in his ball game, or would he continue to play by himself, not wanting human interaction? After a few minutes, he stopped, his feet splayed, ready to run with the ball firmly clamped in his mouth. He watched me to see if I was going to call him over or try to chase him. Most likely, this was how he played with his former owner, so ignoring him, I turned around and walked away. He ran for a few more minutes, trying to entice me to chase him, but when I would not, he brought the ball over, dropping it at my feet. I took the leash off, telling him to sit. He sat with his eyes on the ball, barking. He expected me to pick his prized possession up to throw for him. To reward him for sitting and including me in his ball game nicely, I picked up the ball and threw it.

He was happy and excited as he chased after it, quickly picking it up. Next, he sprinted to the other side of the yard, dropping the ball between his paws. He eagerly waited to see my reaction. Again, I turned my back on him and walked in the opposite direction. He picked up the ball and barreled past me, trying to get my attention, but when I ignored him, he became uncertain and stopped. He was unsure how this new ball game was to be played, but then, with the sheer joy of wanting to chase his ball, he ran towards me, placing it at my feet. Backing up, he sat, ready for the next throw. At that moment, I knew he didn't care about the rules of the ball game, he just wanted to play, and he agreed to any rules I set.

His last owner had probably chased him while yelling his name, trying to get him to come, and when he would not release the ball, he most likely tried to wrestle it out of his mouth. This gave Gizmo full control of how the game was to be played. He would not listen or come, and the playtime was a chaotic, frustrating experience for the owner. I refused to play the game his way, and by setting new rules, he complied, bringing the ball over to me. If he wanted to play, he had to play my way, with my rules.

Walking him was not much better for the owner, because Gizmo would jerk on the leash, dragging him wherever Gizmo wanted to go. These behaviors were all learned, which worked well for Gizmo but did not make walking him enjoyable or safe. This would also have to change before he could be adopted.

After we played for a while, I tried to call him over to take him to my office to evaluate him, but when he saw the leash in my hand, he knew we were going back indoors. This he did not want to do, so instead of coming, he joyfully ran away from me, not wanting to stop the ball game. I stood watching him run from me in gleeful madness. I knew he was smart, but what he didn't know was that I had dealt with his kind before, and he had just met his match.

Walking over to the picnic table, I reached into a bucket to get another ball. As soon as he saw me holding it, he rushed towards me, dropping the ball from his mouth right at my feet. I threw the new ball for him, picking up the old one. We played this back-and-forth rapid-fire game for about seven minutes. When he was panting and needed a rest, I picked up the released ball he had just dropped, and with his attention on the ball, I slipped the loose leash over his head. With his full attention on the ball in my hand, we walked calmly and quietly back to my office.

I had learned over the years I could do anything with a ball-driven dog, as long as they could see the ball. While Gizmo and I had already started our training journey, I understood if his new adopters didn't understand this important trick, it would result in failure for both the dog and the owner. The ball was Gizmo's reward, and he would do just about anything to have it.

Once in my office, Gizmo continued to focus on the ball, wanting me to throw it for him every time he laid it at my feet or put it in my lap. He was not curious about looking around the room or interested in the food dish I set before him; he was obsessed with the ball. When I body-handled him to see if he would react, he stood over the ball, mesmerized, his nose inches above it like a transfixed stuffed animal. Finally, to see what he would do, I picked the ball up and walked out of the room, leaving him behind.

I had a small window in the door I could watch him through. He came out of his ball hypnosis state, hunting for it everywhere.

I walked down the hall for a few minutes, and when I returned, I looked in to see him on top of my file cabinet, rummaging through a basket. Entering the room, he jumped down, begging me for the ball.

While I was gone, he had rearranged everything in my office, leaving no space unturned, but he had not found his beloved ball. I tried to continue with the evaluation, but if I did not have the ball in my hand, waving it in front of him, I could not get his attention. Showing it to him again, he sat like a gentleman, his body trembling in anticipation, wanting me to throw it. I wanted to see if he was familiar with any additional commands, so I asked him to lie down. Not taking his eyes off the ball, he slowly lowered his body to the floor.

"Good boy," I praised him.

I moved the ball towards my head, then moved it back out at arm's length, with his eyes following the ball. As I slowly moved the ball back towards my head, I said to him, "Look at me." When he looked at me, I rewarded him by throwing the ball. Repeating this movement and command several times, he soon learned what I wanted from him. Again, he was delighted with this new game, and after he chased the ball, he would bring it over, dropping it at my feet. But now he was giving me eye contact. He still ran after the ball in a crazed state of mind and was not mindful of things around him. In his evaluation, I made a note stating he wouldn't be a good fit as a family dog or for a senior person, as his tendency to plow into things might cause them being knocked over.

This was a concern for me because it limited what kind of home he could go into, narrowing the application candidates. I needed to know what he would do if a person was in the room with him and the ball suddenly disappeared, so I picked it up, threw it into the hallway, and closed the door. He ran to the door, smelling along the bottom, trying to get its scent. Once he scented it, he barked and scratched on the door. When he could not get it open, he dug at the linoleum on the floor. He knew the ball was in the hall, and frantic to get to it, he dug at the sheetrock on the wall next to the door, tearing a hole in it. I knew at this point he was going to be very hard to adopt out. In addition, I knew I would need to bring in a trainer who might work with him. I called him over and took out another ball from my file cabinet. With the ball in my hand, I placed the loose leash over his head and we walked back to his kennel.

"She is a miracle worker," I heard the staff saying as we walked past the front desk. "What a difference from this morning! Look how well he is walking beside her now."

Little did they know it was the magic of the ball, and without it, Gizmo would be in full chaotic form. After putting Gizmo in his kennel, I went back to my office. I pushed a small cabinet in front of the damaged sheetrock and sat down to place a call to a trainer named Theresa.

If anyone deserves admiration in this world, it would be Theresa. Not only was she the best trainer I have ever met, but she had also overcome adversity with a determined toughness and grit, wearing a banner of courage which gave her special strength. She had been a nurse, taught at a nearby college, and in her late forties, had lost both her legs. For her, it was another battle to conquer and overcome, so she battled on. She strapped on her prosthetic legs, called running blades, and accomplished what she loved most: training difficult dogs. They became her students, and she demanded a lot from them. Her goal was to get them adopted or into a working situation. When she was training a particular dog, we would post a sign on their kennel door stating the dog was in training with Theresa.

"Do not take out."

People did not mess with Theresa, and neither did the dogs.

Theresa and I had become a team. When I called her, she would come to the shelter, and we would sit at my desk strategizing on how to train the dog I was concerned about. We would formulate a plan to get him into the best adoptable or working situation. Theresa was in my office the next day after I made the call to her. I told her about Gizmo's history and what I had discovered about him. We walked to his kennel for her to meet him. He did the same routine as he had the day before, except now I had a ball in my hand, and he wanted it, so he was on his best behavior.

I left her with him, warning her of his out-of-control manners unless he saw a ball. About ten minutes later, they walked quietly by my office, with Gizmo walking well on the leash. Theresa, with a smile, gave me a thumbs up, showing me the ball in her hand. Gizmo, though excited, had his eyes on his adored ball and was behaving. I sat restlessly, tapping my pen on the desktop, waiting for her to return. Finally, the door opened, and with quiet instructions, she released Gizmo into the room. He immediately started searching my office for another ball.

Sitting down, Theresa said, "I agree with you; this big guy is going to be hard to adopt out."

Gizmo spotted a ball under the Kuranda bed and was trying to crawl under it to reach it. Theresa looked at me, saying, "He is not going to do well in the shelter environment because there is no consistency here. He will just regress, becoming more unbalanced than he already is, so I need to take him home to foster him for a couple of weeks."

At this point, Gizmo had retrieved his ball, dropping it in the water bowl, spilling water onto the floor. We looked at each other, shaking our heads.

"I'm going to take him back to his kennel, and then let's go talk to your director and explain what is going on with him."

I liked it when Theresa would take dogs home. They learned great skills and manners, which helped them to get adopted. She also had the opportunity to evaluate the dog in a home setting and see what kind of home they would best fit into. After talking to our director, we loaded Gizmo into Theresa's car for two weeks of doggy boot camp.

I did not hear back from Theresa for three weeks, and then a knock came on my door with Theresa stepping into my office.

"Where is Gizmo?" I asked, looking behind her.

"Oh, he's still at home," she said with a smile that turned to a frown. "Julie, I think we are setting him up for failure if we try to put him into a normal household."

Looking intently at me, she said, "This is a working dog who wants to work. I think we should call Boeing and see if we can get him into their K9 Unit Program."

I had been having the same thoughts about putting him into a working environment, but I needed a second opinion before trying to find a placement for him.

Theresa leaned up against the doorframe. "If Boeing has an opening, it would be great, and if they don't, I will try to keep him until they do."

She handed me Boeing's number and left. I had not worked with Boeing before, but I had heard great things about their K9 program. I placed the call, leaving a message, telling them who we were and about Gizmo. Hanging up, I waited for them to call me back, and the next morning, the call came in. They told me they had some openings in their kennels and were looking for dogs. They were interested in coming up to meet Gizmo and made an appointment for the coming Thursday.

On Thursday afternoon, a Boeing dog handler came to the shelter to meet and evaluate Gizmo. She introduced herself, and Theresa turned Gizmo over to her so she could start evaluating him. She walked him to the play yard, and we followed close behind. Gizmo was excited and wanted to play. He was pulling on the leash, but she did not correct him, telling us they wanted their dogs to be out front. In the play yard, Gizmo immediately started running to search for a ball. Calling him over, she pulled a ball out of her pocket. He sat down in front of her, giving her great eye contact. She talked to him in an excited voice, putting the ball in his mouth to get his scent on it. Then, throwing the ball for him, she watched as he ran after it, snatching it up.

During this playtime, she played a game of tug-of-war, telling him to drop the ball so she could see if he would release it on command. Then she walked away from him, watching to see if he would follow her or lose interest. After playing with him for a while, she walked by me, handing me the ball, and taking another ball out of her pocket, she instructed me to hide them both in different places. While I hid the balls, she distracted Gizmo by pulling another ball out of her pocket. Once I had hidden them, she waved the ball in her hand, pretending to throw it while instructing Gizmo to find it. Excited, he ran towards where he thought he had seen her throw, but not seeing the ball, he looked back at her.

"Get the ball," she told him.

He started running, searching with his nose to the ground. Soon he spotted one of the balls I had hidden, but when he reached it, he ran past it, not interested, and was still looking for the other ball. I was disappointed he had left the ball, but she seemed confident while she watched him. Running and searching around the yard, Gizmo finally raised his nose in the air, getting a scent of the other ball. Head held high, he followed his nose to where the second ball had been hidden. Grabbing the ball, he happily ran around the yard, shaking his head, and running back, he dropped it at her feet.

"Good boy," she said, praising him.

She turned and looked at us. "He brought back the ball that had his scent on it."

I looked at the ball she held up.

"The other ball had a red X on it," she said. "It was the ball that did not have his scent on it. He found the right ball."

We did the search routine several times, hiding the ball in harder places. Gizmo found the right ball every time. He loved this new game and would not stop searching until he located the ball. Bringing it back, he would back up and sit, wanting to continue the game. Finally, she picked the ball up, throwing it over the gate. Gizmo ran after it but was stopped by the fence. He could see it on the other side but could not reach it. Running back and forth, he started to dig, frustrated it was out of his reach. Finally, he stopped and sat down, barking, wanting us to open the gate.

She looked at us, smiling. "We'll take him. I think he will work in our K9 program." Watching Gizmo, she said, "We will keep you posted. If he fails, we will have to bring him back."

Theresa smiled as we walked up to the office to do the paper-work. When we watched them drive away, Theresa and I felt confident Gizmo was on his way to a new life. With his nose and drive, we hoped he would pass the course, becoming a working K9 who would serve his community, state, or country.

Theresa and I talked several times during the next month, hoping Gizmo would not fail the training program he had been placed in. Finally, we heard from Boeing. Gizmo had passed. After training, he had earned his badge as a bomb dog and was now placed with a handler. We both knew Gizmo would be able to work where he would be happy. As the years passed, we would occasionally hear how he was doing. He became one of the top K9 bomb dogs in this state. He worked ten years before he was retired, and I could ask most police officers if they had met Gizmo or heard of him, and many of them had.

Through the years, I have sent other dogs to Boeing for K9 training for drugs or bombs, and I am proud of them all, but Gizmo was my first. Theresa died before she knew all of Gizmo's accomplishments, which made me sad. A year before I retired, I was contacted and told Gizmo had passed away. I am so proud of him and so glad I was able to work with Theresa, who had helped so many dogs. They both accomplished so much, giving to their community, both saving lives. What a legacy these two have left us, with great memories and love for them both.

I say, "Goodbye, my friends, and well done."

"Service dog's don't just change the lives of their handlers; they change the world."

AUTHOR UNKNOWN

MARS AND BABIE

If you have ever owned a Great Dane, you know you are in the presence of royalty. Great Danes are dignified, elegant, and very large, often weighing between one hundred to one hundred and twenty pounds. Most of the time, they have a very good temperament, but their imposing size can be intimidating. They are almost goofy while playing, taking long, loping strides, their feet pounding on the ground as they run, with their heavy jowls flapping. Their bursts of energy do not last long, and they will settle to the ground, pushing back into their haunches, head high, front feet crossed, for a rest to watch you.

When I heard animal control had brought in a Dane and another dog, I assumed they were both Danes. I hurried back to meet them after being told they were in the East Wing, in kennels 15 and 16. I hated Pod F, where these kennels are, because the lights are sometimes hard to turn on, and it was no different on this morning. Going through the door, I messed with the light switch, cursing when it would not turn on. While I was flicking the switch on and off, I heard from behind me a low rumbling growl, followed by a full, deep-throated explosive roar. Jumping, I spun around, and there stood the largest Dane I had ever seen, glaring at me. He was so black he blended in with the blackness of the kennel; his white teeth were showing out of the rage of his face, and he was mad. His menacing height put him in a position of looking at me eye to eye, and I am sure if he could have reached me, he would have torn me limb to limb. I knew the kennel stood between us, but it took me a moment to get over the fear this brute had caused. I hesitantly reached up to turn his paperwork over so I could read it, and at that moment, he lunged, hitting the bars with such force that the sound reverberated around the room. Shaken, I tried to speak softly to him, and he settled some, but continued to pace around his kennel like a roaring lion. Reading his placard, it said his name was Mars.

"How in the world did animal control get you in here?" I thought. Standing there, I wondered how we were going to handle him safely if we had to. Now that it was a little quieter, I heard a soft whine from the kennel beside him. Leaning over, I looked in, expecting to see another Dane, but there sat a small, petite Pitbull. She, too, was all black, but her countenance was exactly the opposite of Mars. She sat quietly, her tail moving in a swishing movement behind her, wiping the floor with her friendliness. Her eyes sparkled with good-natured affection, and she actually seemed apologetic for Mars's unacceptable behavior. Kneeling down, I greeted her while her dark brown eyes charmed me as she reached out to lick my fingers. I stood to read her paperwork, which said her name was Babie.

"Hi Babie," I said, petting her with my fingers through the bars. "Let's take you out for a walk, but bad boy Mars can stay where he is until he is nicer."

She jumped in happiness while I leashed her up, and we left for a walk. Mars looked happy when he saw Babie, but at seeing me, he once again displayed his toothy weapons.

A couple of days went by with Mars's behavior not improving, but Babie became the star of the staff, loving everyone with her congenial personality. While Mars roared, Babie threw kisses through her kennel bars to anyone who walked past her. The shelter has always allowed visitors into the kennel area to meet the dogs, but it soon became a problem with Pod F. After visitors went into Mars and Babie's pod, they made a beeline to the front desk, informing us of the aggressive dog. The staff would explain to them we could not handle Mars, so it was impossible to move him to the North Wing. It would have been better for Mars in the North Wing because it was quieter, with less foot traffic and no visitors, but we couldn't handle him to move him. Then their concern would turn to Babie. They would wonder why we did not move her. We told them we did not want to move Babie because both dogs came in together, and she helped to comfort him. They still did not like the answers we gave them, so after a couple of days, we made the choice to lock the doors, closing Pod F to visitors. This gave Mars a reprieve and kept the public safe, but there was hell to pay for anyone who looked through the window in the door. We always knew when they did because Mars's booming bark roared forth, and we could hear it at the front desk.

A week after the two dogs had been brought in, I was at the front desk filling out paperwork when someone opened the front door. The metallic tinkling and jingle of bracelets reached my ears. I looked up but could see no one until I heard a clearing of the throat on the other side of the counter. I stood up, bending forward to look, and a tiny old woman met my eyes. She looked at me through her snapping dark brown, wizened eyes. Each eyelid had turquoise eye shadow spread across them, and her eyebrows were carefully penciled in. She carefully applied pink rouge to her brown, prunish cheeks, and she used the same pink color to cover her lips. She dyed her long, curly hair black, and it flared out in all directions. She wore huge hoop earrings dangling from each ear, and they were the size of one of her bangled bracelets. Her dress was a turquoise muumuu that matched her eye shadow, and it swept the floor with its hem. It was belted with a gold-colored cord with tiny silver bells attached to the tassels.

"I am Amella, and I've come to get my rikano, how you say, dogs," she said in broken English.

Still looking on in wonder, I asked who her dogs were. "Mars and Babie, they are my dogs."

Surprised, I said, "Mars and Babie are your dogs?"

"Dah, dah, they are my dogs," she jingled back at me, waving a paper through the air. "I have a release from the animal control," she said, slapping down the release papers on the counter. "You give them back to me?"

Grabbing the piece of paper up, I told her, "I will be right back."

Tapping on the director's door, I went in with a puzzled expression. She looked at me over the clutter on her desk.

"You need to come out front and see this," I said, puzzled. "There is an older woman who is claiming to be the owner of Mars and Babie."

She stood up and walked to the door to peek out. "Is that Amella?" she said, smiling.

"Yes, that is the name she gave me."

Laughing, she said, "Animal control called me this morning to inform me that Mars and Babie's owner would come to get them. She has fixed her fence so they can't escape again and paid her fine, so we are to release them to her."

Standing there watching Amella, she whispered back at me, "You never know who is going to walk through those doors each day. Don't you love the variety of people in this world?"

Smiling, and with a touch of guilt, I said, "They certainly put a smile on your face." Then, looking at her with concern, I said, "Who is going to get Mars out? No one here can handle him."

Sitting down behind her desk, she rearranged the piles of papers. "Have Pat do the paperwork, then after Amella has signed them, she can go back with you to get Mars out."

I have to admit, at that moment; I had a feeling of dread, not wanting to be anywhere close to Mars once he was loose. I knew if he charged, this tiny little woman could not hold him back. Leaving the director's office, I called Pat up to the front desk, enjoying her surprised look as she gazed at Amella, who patiently stood waiting for help.

"Amella, this is Pat, and she is going to have you sign some paperwork while I get Babie for you," I said, picking up a leash. "Mars has been very naughty, and he will let no one near him, so we are going to have you come back with us to get him out."

She gazed at me intently. "What? Mars is a good boy to me."

Walking away, I said, "Well, he doesn't like anyone here. I'll be right back with Babie." I was relieved we would not have to put up with Mars's aggression or have to handle him. This gave me a moment to decide how she could get him out and also gave me time to plan a way to keep myself safe. I slid by Mars's kennel as he warned me with his booming voice. Entering Babie's kennel, she wagged her tail with cheerfulness while I put her leash on. We walked to the front counter to reunite her with Amella. The minute she spotted her, she barked with delight, wiggling and squirming to get to her. Amella went to her knees, hugging Babie.

"Oh, my Babie chey, your Dya has missed you."

She hugged Babie as Babie lathered her face in kisses. Together, we walked out to her car, and she opened the back door for Babie to jump into. "You stay," she told Babie. Babie sat down with her head hanging out the window. Walking back into the shelter, she pulled a rolled-up rope from her dress pocket. We entered the kennel area, and Mars was in full ferocity, displaying his temper at our entrance, but when he heard Amella's voice, he stopped, giving a low whimper. His tail went down with small waves, and he swayed on his front feet, his head lowered. He looked as if he was making homage to a queen, bowing down before her with relief in his eyes at seeing her.

She looked at Mars, frowning, and shook her bangled hand at him. "Mars, you are bi-lacho, no good; you act dili, crazy rikano dog." She frowned, clicking her tongue at him. "You should be lashav, shame, shame," she said, scolding him.

By now, Mars's head was hanging down dejectedly, his tail completely tucked under his body. She stood there with the rope in her hand while I unlocked the kennel door. Stepping in, she again shook her hand at him. "Get down, Mars," she scolded.

Mars immediately dropped to the floor and licked her hand while she scratched the top of his head. "Why you be bad to these friends? They are good to you," she crooned to him in a soft voice while putting the rope over his head. "Good rikano, Dya missed you," she said, petting and kissing him. Finally, she straightened up. "We come out now," she said, opening the kennel door.

I stepped behind the pod door for safety, not wanting to take a chance of any confrontation with Mars. Holding the rope in her hand, she led a submissive, docile dog out the door and down the hall. I followed a short distance behind them, watching as they ambled up the hallway. Watching them, I had the extraordinary view of this old tiny woman with full control of this massive dog. As we walked to the front door, several staff members joined in walking behind them. We all watched in wonder and admiration at this image. Following her out to the parking lot, she opened the door of her car, instructing Mars to get in. Jumping inside the car, he was happy and excited to be reunited with Babie, while his enormous bulk covered most of the back seat of Amella's little car.

"Thank you, my friends," Amella said, walking around to the driver's side of her car. "See, he is a good boy, my Mars is."

Wrinkling her prunish face with a smile, she got into her car. A staff member elbowed me, pointing at Mars, who looked back at us, showing a full set of bared teeth as his final farewell. When Amella drove off, we could see two happy, contented dogs, with both their heads out the back windows. Babie's ears laid back with joy, while Mars's jowls flapped in the breeze. Out of the driver's window came a brown, leathered arm covered with sparkling bangles, waving goodbye.

"All dogs are good, some are just a little ruff around the edges."

AUTHOR UNKNOWN

VINNEY

There is only one way to describe a Jack Russell Terrier: strong-willed, determined, and intelligent. They are a popular breed, but they require a strong and determined owner who will manage the Jack Russell's indomitable, scrappy behavior. These little dogs have a big dog personality. Many new owners are charmed by these adorable little dogs, but soon realize Jack Russells have high energy levels and can easily take control of the household. They make wonderful companions for the right owners, but they require regular exercise as part of their everyday routine.

Unfortunately, many Jack Russells end up in shelters because their previous owners became discouraged, not understanding the breed's unique needs. Thankfully, their stay is usually brief, as people who understand Jack Russells adore them.

Vinney, a Parson Jack Russell, came to the shelter after being abandoned in an apartment building with another dog. He had a white wire-haired coat spotted with a few patches of brown and black, with the same brown covering his ears and running down to his black eyes. A blaze of white ran down the middle of his forehead to his white whiskered muzzle, showing off his black nose. Walking with a swagger, he wagged his short stub tail like a metronome. Friendly and lighthearted, Vinney quickly endeared himself to all the staff. Once he became available for adoption, he attracted a lot of interest from people who love the Jack Russell breed.

Because he was a stray, we had very little information on him, so it was important to learn as much as we could before finding him the right home. After his evaluation, we knew we had to place him in a home which could keep up with his high energy needs.

On a beautiful, sunny day, I went to get Vinney for his evaluation. We went outside for playtime and a walk. In his excitement, he jumped beside me as if he had springs in his legs. He ran, whirling with random delight, until he dropped, panting and loving the fresh green grass as he rolled in it. On our walk, I discovered Vinney loved other dogs and cats, but especially, he loved people. When we reached my office, he looked around with pleasure, probing under things. He investigated every nook and cranny, his little nose not missing anything. Then, satisfied, he found a squeaky toy in the toy box, rolling on the floor and loving the squeak, squeak, squeak sound it made as he wrestled with it. Now a prized possession, he took it to his bed and hid it under a blanket for safekeeping.

During the evaluation, he was content to lie on his bed, squeaking his new toy. When he was tired of playing, he laid his head down on his front paws and observed me with his keen black eyes. After a few moments, he came over and jumped onto the chair beside my desk. He sat there motionless, his butt rooted to the chair, watching as I worked on the computer. Emmi knocked on my office door and stepped in. Kneeling down, she picked up Vinney's squeaky toy from his bed and threw it for him. Barking with delight, he flew off the chair to retrieve it.

"I came in because I can't find an old evaluation record on a dog," she said. "I know you keep copies of them in your file cabinet."

Opening the cabinet, we both searched through the files for the missing record.

"Here it is," I said, handing it to her.

We stood talking for a few minutes, and then she knelt down, cupping Vinney's head in her hands. "You're such a good boy, Vinney."

After she left, I turned back to my desk and reached down for my pen, but it was not there. I picked up some papers, looking under them, but it wasn't there either. Thinking I had dropped it, I bent down to look under the desk, and out of the corner of my eye, I saw Vinney busily burying something in his bed. I walked over to watch as he pushed the blanket over a prized possession with his nose. Lifting a corner of the blanket, I found my pen. Laughing, I recovered it and went back to work while Vinney happily chewed on his toy.

Later, I was called to the front desk, and as I was leaving, I looked back at Vinney. "You be a good boy," I said, pocketing my pen. When I returned, I found Vinney lying on his bed with his toy, acting sleepy and content. When I sat down to work, I immediately noticed someone had rummaged through my desk. Missing were the scotch tape, another pen, and a collar which had been lying there.

"You little thief," I said, laughing.

Vinney looked up at me with innocent, saintly eyes. Amused, I continued playing his little game by placing things on my desk while he watched me. When I turned away, acting busy, he jumped from his bed to the chair, then onto the top of my desk, snatching his new loot. Running back, he buried it under his blanket. I decided Vinney's name fit him perfectly. In a past life, he must have belonged to the mob, or perhaps he had rubbed shoulders with Bonnie and Clyde. Laughing, I continued our little game until Emmi knocked on my door again.

"I think I may have left my pen in here," she said, still searching through her pockets. "Have you seen it?"

Without looking up, I pointed to Vinney's bed. "It's under his blankets with all my stuff."

She laughed as she dug through his stolen treasures, coming up with her pen.

"Wow, you've got quite a booty here," she said. "Whatever you do, Julie, don't leave your purse lying around."

Giving Vinney a farewell pat on the head, she waved at me from the door.

A few days later, our director went through the applications and chose a family she felt would be a good fit for Vinney. She called the Petersons, planning for them to come and meet him. On a Saturday afternoon, the Peterson family—mom, dad, and two kids—came for their appointment. We put them in an office while a staff member went to get Vinney.

Their daughter, Rose, was around the age of fourteen and dressed in a gothic style. She wore a black dress with black net stockings, and her black army-style boots laced around her ankles. She dyed her hair black, with a purple streak running across her forehead and covering her right eye. When her parents tried to engage her, she would look up from her phone, casually toss her head, and roll her eyes. It was obvious she did not want to be at the shelter to see a dog.

Their son, Ben, was around the age of seven. He had bright red hair with freckles across his nose and face. His bright blue eyes were expressive, and his excitement at meeting Vinney was palpable. He wore jeans and a plaid shirt with a bright red Spiderman cape flapping behind him.

When they brought Vinney in, Ben fell before him, nose to nose, and said in an animated voice, "Hello, Vinney."

Vinney, with a friendly quiver of his tail, wagged a hello back. Picking up a toy, Ben threw it across the room, and Vinney, thrilled, gave chase, hunting it down and bringing it back to him. Ben laughed as he rolled on the floor with Vinney, who made playful growls. Grabbing his cape, Vinney pulled on it, playing a game of tug-of-war, making Ben laugh even harder. As they played, even Rose laughed at Vinney's antics and charming behavior. Watching their kids enjoy this funny little dog, the parents knew Vinney would be a great fit for their family. They asked a few more questions and then completed the adoption.

Once they signed the paperwork, they prepared to leave. We took their first family pictures, with Vinney happily posing on Ben's lap. With cheerful smiles, the staff clapped and cheered as Vinney went home with his new family.

We heard nothing about Vinney for a couple of months until fall. The leaves were turning a crisp orange and yellow, and winter was fast approaching. On a cool October day, we received a call from the Petersons—they were bringing Vinney in for a visit. We were all excited to see them, and when they arrived, they were eager to share stories of Vinney's comical ways and amusing behaviors. They raved about how much they loved Vinney and how he had become a favorite new citizen in their town. They told us how he swaggered up and down the sidewalks, poking his nose into shops and expecting treats from the shop owners.

Just before they were ready to leave, the dad turned around and said, "Vinney has a very unusual quirk."

"Oh?" I asked, giving Vinney a last pat.

With a bewildered grin, he began, "He steals things."

He stared at me. "We started missing things around the house, and the kids were fighting, accusing each other of taking one another's belongings."

Looking at Vinney, I asked, "What had gone missing?"

"Oh," he said. "Lipstick, nail polish, toy cars, sandals, money, utensils, eyeglasses, mail... But then, one day, my wife's phone went missing, and we all searched everywhere for it. We tore the house apart but couldn't find it anywhere. She had put her phone on vibrate, so we couldn't hear it ringing."

"Where was Vinney while all this was taking place?" I asked.

He smiled. "Oh! That's the funny part—Vinney sat on his bed, watching the whole thing. Finally, when Rose got close to his bed, she heard a muffled buzzing coming from beneath his derriere."

Standing there holding Vinney, he continued, "She reached down to pick him up, and looking under his blanket, there was the stolen phone, plus all the other contraband the kids had been missing and fighting about."

I started laughing. "I'm so sorry. I forgot to tell you he's a bit of a thief."

"Well," he continued, "with the crimes being solved, we at least know who the culprit is. When things go missing, we shake out his bed. So far, it's the only place he has hidden things."

With a twinkle in his eye, he added, "We've also learned to check his bed before guests leave because his thieving doesn't exclude family members only, and he loves car keys."

By then, we were all laughing while Vinney wagged his tail, his innocent face showing no remorse for looting his new family's belongings. In his mind, their things were his fortunes and treasures, newfound wealth, which he happily deposited for safekeeping under his blanket.

Smiling, the mom said, "He has been a great addition to our home."

Ben reached over, taking Vinney from his dad. "We love him —he's the best," he said.

I gave Vinney a final pet and watched them get into their car to drive away. I was still laughing at all the stories they had told me, happy Vinney had found such a great home. After a last wave, I walked back into the shelter. Then, stopping, I reached into my pocket to see if my pen was still there. It was.

"Dog's have a way of finding joy in the simplest things, like a stick or a tennis ball."

AUTHOR UNKNOWN

SOCKET

The Border Collie is one of the most beautiful dogs; it is also one of the more complicated breeds. Highly intelligent with a strong work drive, this breed requires a job. People who own them need to provide activities for their dog that will help with physical and mental stimulation. They are a very loyal breed, and in the Border's mind, their person is the source of affection, a job, and a partner. Whether it is herding or agility, if they don't have a job to do, they can become fixated on other things, such as the running feet of children or the moving wheels of a passing car. These movements can trigger their natural herding instinct, becoming an outlet for their pent-up energy. I always say, a happy Border is a busy Border.

They are affectionate with their family but usually reserved with strangers. Though they look like a cute, cuddly dog, they prefer to be left alone to do their job. The Scottish Highland Games are an event which comes to the Valley every year. Many people become interested in owning a Border Collie after witnessing their impressive sheep herding abilities, but they often underestimate the time commitment required to care for a herding dog. This leads to a frustrated dog and a frustrated person. New owners may find themselves doing repairs on their house after the Border decides his new home needs remodeling, with him being the demolition crew.

I don't care for the cold here in the Northwest. Growing up in Montana, it could get well below zero, but you can layer with enough sweaters, coats, scarves, and mittens to stay warm. Here, we are nestled between the ocean and the mountains, where the valleys hold on to the cool, damp air. It is a very different cold; it wraps around you like a wet blanket, pushing deep into your bones and chilling you to your inner core.

I was complaining loudly as I turned up the heat in my car while driving to work on a chilly January morning. The mist lay on the farm ground, creeping toward me with its damp fingers. Beautiful to look at, it is unrelenting, making it hard to stay warm. Walking into the shelter, I clapped my hands together, trying to warm my numb fingers. Pat greeted me with the announcement that they had brought in a Border Collie the day before.

"He's a mean one," she stated while shoving papers around the front desk, upset by the way people had left it the night before.

"What's his story?" I asked, searching the desk for his paperwork.

"They abandoned him at the Brown Motel," she said, her voice growing louder. "They rent rooms out to people for a month at a time, and this guy had been staying there for a while, working on the new bridge. The lady who brought the dog told us he had left a few days ago and did not return. When they went to check on his room, they found everything gone except his dog with a big bowl of food."

Slapping more papers around, she continued. "They had quite a time getting him because he would not come to anyone and was trying to bite them. They finally got him and brought him here." By now, she was flinging papers everywhere while continuing in a cross voice. "I can't believe someone would drive off and leave their dog behind."

Removing my hat and coat, I picked up his paperwork, reading it as I walked to my office. It said he was five years old, neutered, and his name was Socket. They sure seemed to know a lot about him, I thought, puzzled. Our staff had noted he was hard to handle upon intake, which didn't surprise me since he was a Border. They rarely care for a stranger touching or handling them.

Sitting down at my desk, I pushed the paperwork aside, dreading my first meeting with Socket since I would have to take him outdoors in the cold. I put my coat and hat back on, grabbing my gloves, and picking up a loop leash, I headed for the dog runs. Whether or not he liked it, he needed to go outdoors where it was less stressful. Outside, he could go to the bathroom and then a nice walk.

I went into the dog runs, looking into kennel 16. Laying on his bed was a very unhappy Border Collie.

"Good morning, Socket," I said.

His ears pricked forward as he recognized his name, but seeing it was a stranger talking to him, he responded with a low growl. Carefully opening the door, I went in. "Can I come in with you, my friend?" I said. "You need to go out and go potty."

I walked a little closer to see what his response would be. He growled a little louder but did not show teeth. I took the leash, dangling it in front of him while he sat up, firmly planting his body in the corner. By his body language, I knew he would not lunge at me, so I carefully placed the loop over his head, gently pulling it tight. Knowing he was on the lead, he submitted. I crooned to him, talking in a soft voice, telling him what a good boy he was.

He was a typical Border Collie, black with a white bib running down his chest and continuing down both front legs. His back legs had white socks, and his tail had the usual

Border Collie tuck with the familiar white tip. He had a blaze of white running down his forehead between his brown, intelligent eyes, stopping at his black nose. Walking with me to the outside door, he sat like a gentleman, waiting for me to open it.

Surprised, I said, "Well, you've had some training; what a smart boy you are."

I knew better than to touch him, but I could tell he liked to be praised. We took a brisk walk around the property so he could smell everything and relieve himself. He began to relax, but still continued to look back, watching me closely with suspicion. Taking him back to my office, I carefully slipped the leash off. He looked around the room in a noncommittal way, avoiding me. If I tried to coax him over, he gave a warning growl, telling me to keep my distance.

Preparing some food, I set the bowl down on the floor, hoping he would eat. He walked over to smell it, but instead of eating, he pushed the bowl under the Kuranda bed with his nose.

Smiling, I said, "I'm not that easily defeated."

Sitting down, I pretended to be busy with other things while he laid down on the floor by the door, watching me. Every once in a while, I would get up and move around the room, keeping my movements slow. He kept growling, clearly establishing a boundary I knew not to cross.

Around lunchtime, I was feeling hungry, so I took my peanut butter and jelly sandwich out of my lunch box. When I pulled it out of the sandwich bag, his tail started thumping rhythmically on the floor. Watching his new demeanor, I took a bite.

"Oh, you're a bum," I said, chewing.

I broke off a piece and offered it to him, and he extended his neck to take it. While he belly crawled closer, I took a few more bites until he finally sat beside me. With his ears pricked forward, he begged for food. If I withheld a piece, he would sit up on his haunches, waving his paws in the air. Giving him the last morsel, I moved my hand slowly toward him, and he submitted to my touch.

"I know how to win a man's heart," I said. "Can we be friends now?"

Touching him gently around his head, I watched for a reaction while trying to assure him all would be well. At that moment, I did not realize how seriously he would take the question about being friends because, in his mind, I had not only become his friend but also his new job.

A knock sounded on my door, and Kevin, a shelter volunteer, came in. Socket immediately moved to the back of the room, growling at him.

"This fellow is going to need a lot of work," I told him. "Would you be willing to walk him?"

Kevin gently nodded his head. "If he will let me, I can take him out on the days you're not here."

I coaxed Socket over to me. "My hope is he will get used to other people handling him."

I knew if anyone could make up with Socket, it would be Kevin. He had a quiet way with dogs that made them feel comfortable. I put the leash back on Socket so we could take him for another walk outdoors. While we walked together, I handed the leash to Kevin. I could tell Socket was distrustful of him, but we continued to walk, and he relaxed, enjoying being back outdoors.

When we had come back to the dog runs, I said, "Oh, by the way, he loves peanut butter and jelly sandwiches."

Kevin smiled. "I think I can arrange that."

I put Socket back in his kennel, taking the leash off. Stepping out, I locked the gate behind me, and we watched Socket unhappily lay down on his bed.

"If he doesn't become friendlier, he will be very hard to adopt out."

Kevin patted me on the back. "Give him some time."

Kevin worked with Socket for several days, taking him for long walks. Socket still focused on me, but got used to Kevin handling him. He continued to growl and was cranky with other staff members and volunteers if they tried to go in with him.

One day, as I was working with another dog, I heard Pat on the intercom asking if I could come to the front desk. When I got there, I noticed three staff members with their backs to me, looking toward the front door. Hearing my footsteps, they parted like the Red Sea, and there, sitting outside, was Socket, looking in.

Surprised, I said, "How did he get out there?"

"He must have crawled over his outdoor kennel," Pat said. "We tried to catch him, but he ran from us, so you will have to get him since none of us can handle him."

I grabbed a leash and walked to the door to open it. Socket scurried into the shelter like a long-lost friend, greeting me with a gleeful tail wag. I could tell he was excited with his accomplishment, and as I walked him back to his kennel, I scolded him for his behavior.

A half-hour later, he was once again sitting outside the front door, looking in. From that day forward, I was busy retrieving him; back and forth we went, several times a day. On my days off, he would stay in his kennel, not attempting to escape, but on the day I returned, I was constantly hearing,

"Julie, your dog is sitting at the front door. Would you mind coming to get him?"

If the staff tried to catch him, he would delightfully run away from them, loving the game of chase he had created. It was so bad we had to find a safe place for him—not only for his safety but also for visitors who might reach out to grab him as he sat in front of the door. We were worried he might nip or bite someone. For his welfare and our sanity, our director moved him into the barn room at the old building where he could not escape. This troubled me because even though the barn room is a warm, comfortable space, I knew it would not stop Socket's clever mind. We needed to get him to his home or consider a foster situation, but for now, this was the safest place we had for him.

In earnest, we began going through the applications, looking for an experienced owner who could put up with all his Border Collie quirks. One application was interesting, so we placed a call to them. Excited, they wanted to meet him, and the next day they drove to the shelter. They both had recently retired from the corporate world, buying a new home in the valley. With their new freedom, they thought a dog would be a great addition to their new lifestyle.

She was a soft-spoken, tiny woman with a gentle spirit and had owned dogs years ago but never a Border. He was tall with a strong presence and looked at me with intelligent eyes from behind his glasses. He grew up around Border Collies on a ranch in western Wyoming. They quizzed me about Socket, and I asked them many questions, trying to see what their knowledge was of this breed. I needed to know if they had the right skills and energy for Socket.

I walked with them to the big play yard and told them I would bring Socket out for them to meet. When he heard me come into the old building, he was excited, knowing I was there to take him outdoors for his playtime.

Leashing him up, I told him, "There are some nice people here to see you, and I want you to behave yourself."

Giving him a pat on his head, I said, "Please, no silly antics."

We walked outdoors toward the play yard, and it did not take Socket long to discover strangers were present. The closer we got to them, the more he started pulling back on the leash. As we approached the gate, he stopped, and as if on cue, he started barking and jumping like a deranged lunatic on a leash. Wildly flipping and thrashing, he pulled himself free of his collar. Giving me a naughty look—and I swear a smile—he took off running in the opposite direction, ducking and dodging around things. I knew the game he was playing; it was the front door game of catch-me-if-you-can.

Turning, I continued to walk through the gate into the play yard. I knew if I didn't take part, the game would stop. He continued running happily in the opposite direction, but soon noticed I was walking away and not chasing him. He came to a dead stop, and not wanting to be left behind, he flipped around and ran full speed toward the play yard. As he ran through the open gate, I closed it behind him, locking it. As I hung Socket's leash and collar on the fence, I turned and smiled, acting like this was the way we did things around here.

The couple stood there, open-mouthed at the performance they had just seen, and I could tell they didn't think this was normal. We stood there watching Socket while he ran the perimeter of the yard, looking for an escape route.

The man looked at me while shoving his hands into his pockets. "He is a lot of dog. Is he always this wild?"

Socket ran by at full speed while I looked at the man and tried to sound convincing. "He settles down. He stays confined to the old building where there is not a lot of activity, but when he is alone with me, he is great."

We watched Socket sprint around the yard, not interested or curious about the new people with me. Even when they tried to call him over, he ignored them and carried on with carefree indifference. If I moved away from them, he would come over to sit by me, but if they approached him, he would run away to the far perimeters of the fence and bark at them.

Thinking I would try something new, I walked up to the woman to talk to her. While we stood there, Socket stopped to watch us. I could tell he was thinking about what his next move would be when he suddenly spun around and dropped to the stalking position. Then, with a burst of speed, he ran toward us. Just as he reached us, he jumped into the air at shoulder height, flying gracefully between us. As he flew by, he turned his head, looking me straight in the eye. Landing on his feet, he ran back to the far end of the play yard to repeat the same acrobatic feat once again. Then, running a full circle around us, he whipped around and again dropped to the stalking position. Catching his breath, he once more sprinted toward us, but this time he slid to a stop beside me and sat down.

He started barking as if to say, "How did you like that? Pretty cool, huh?"

If a dog could laugh, I was sure he was laughing heartily while he continued to bark.

"I think he is too much dog for us," the man said, frowning.

"We were thinking of a quieter dog with less energy, one who would like to go for a nice, slow walk," the woman said.

Socket continued to bark as the man tried to talk. "He seems to really like you. Have you thought about taking him home?"

I told them it was not possible, and I understood how they felt. I recommended they continue monitoring our website for a suitable dog for their home.

I felt gloomy as we walked back to the old building. I could tell Socket was very pleased with all his impish behaviors, and he had enjoyed his afternoon. Lecturing him on what a naughty boy he was, I put him back in the barn room. While he curled up on his bed, he had a look of satisfaction. I walked over to pet him because how can you stay mad at such a mischievous, roguish dog who just needs a job?

Leaving, I turned and said to him, "Show off."

Sadly, I shut the door behind me. Returning to the new building, everyone looked at me with expectation, hoping Socket had found his new home. Walking into the director's office, I dropped into a chair.

"How did it go?" she asked.

I related the whole incident with some of the staff listening over the half door. By the time I was done, they were all laughing, while I sat there close to tears, knowing Socket was going to be very hard to adopt out.

Sympathetically, my director looked at me. "I have been thinking about this. Let me make a few phone calls, and the rest of you need to get back to work."

I got up to leave, and as I closed her door, I heard her roar with laughter.

Early Tuesday morning, she called me to see if I could come to her office. When I went in, she sat at her desk holding Socket's paperwork.

"You will not believe this," she said, shaking the paperwork at me. "I called the motel to see if they had any information on the man who had left Socket behind. The guy was very grumpy and told me they typically didn't give out personal information, but he would see what he could do."

Looking at me, she continued. "I didn't think I would hear from him, but late yesterday he called me back with the name and phone number of Socket's owner."

Looking intently from across her desk, she continued, "I placed a call to him, leaving a message, and you'll never guess— he called me right back. He couldn't understand why his dog was at our shelter."

I leaned forward to hear what she would say next.

"He told me he had left Socket with a woman friend, and he has been sending her money every month until he had the time to come back for him."

"You have got to be kidding!" I exclaimed.

Setting Socket's file down, she said, "It is the same woman who brought him in."

I sat there, stunned.

"What happens now?" I asked.

She looked at me, smiling. "He wants his dog back."

I was so relieved, I could have danced around her desk.

"He's arranging for some friends to pick him up and take him to the airport, flying him to Denver."

I was so relieved with this news.

"When will that be?" I asked.

"It sounds like it will be on Saturday. They will be here around nine," she said.

Hoping for a happy ending to this saga, we sat at her desk, planning how to safely transfer Socket to the airport and back to his owner.

On Saturday morning, we placed a large white kennel with a bed in it by the front door. I wrote with a red marker all over the kennel: "DO NOT OPEN THIS KENNEL."

I was worried people would not take this ominous warning seriously, so I also placed a large note on top, warning people not to open the kennel. I wrote: "Even if this dog looks distressed, he is an actor, a Houdini, an escape artist," hoping they would heed my warnings.

Eight-thirty rolled around, and Socket's transfer team drove into the shelter parking lot. I walked down to the old building to get Socket and take him for a last walk so he could have some playtime, a good brushing, and some loving pets. At the main building, we loaded him into the travel kennel and zip-tied the door shut, making it secure. The transfer team looked at us dubiously, thinking we had taken extreme measures, and I explained to them that if he got loose in the airport, they would never catch him. I could tell they did not believe me until the man bent over, looking in at Socket with a sympathetic look. Socket, not knowing this man, growled and lunged toward him, acting like a savage beast. The man straightened up, surprised, and assured us Socket would remain in the kennel as long as he was in his care.

I covered his kennel with a sheet, and we loaded him into their van. Watching them drive away, I felt relieved knowing Socket would soon be back with his person.

I waited anxiously all day to hear from Socket's owner,

hoping Socket had arrived safely. Finally, he called. He thanked us for all our efforts and informed us Socket had not changed at all despite the ordeal he had been through. I sat there smiling as I heard Socket's familiar bark.

He continued talking. "He seems like his old self and is over-joyed to see me."

He paused, laughing. "He's happily running through the airport right now."

I sat back in my chair, wondering what "running through the airport" meant, and I wondered if Socket was on a leash?

"Oh well," I thought. "I'm sure Socket would not want to lose sight of his owner ever again."

I paused, thinking. "Or, would he?"

Who knows? It might be interesting to Google the Denver news tonight.

_____

Ingenious, how did my dog ever think of that?

JULIANN BISTRANIN

_____

NOX

Dogs come to the shelter for all kinds of reasons, and at times they are brought to us from animal control, such as Nox was. I walked through the dog runs one morning to see a beautiful full sized German Shepherd laying quietly on his bed. When I stopped in front of his kennel, he looked up at me with inquisitive, intelligent eyes, hoping I was his owner. Seeing I was not, he layed his head back down on his front feet to patiently wait for him.

I knelt down, talking softly to him. "Hey big guy, where did you come from?"

He again looked up, and then with a huge sigh he closed his eyes. Throughout the morning, as staff fed and cleaned he looked up each time someone walked through the door, but not recognizing his person, he laid his head back down with a gentle resolve to quietly wait.

I love the German Shepherd breed with their intelligent, loyal nature. They are a beautiful dog that carries themselves with confidence. Because they are so intelligent they are easy to train. Understanding pack order, they want their trainer to be as confident as they are. When I bring a German Shepherd into my room, they all do the same behavior. Sitting by my door they observe me, trying to understand who I am, and what skills I have. Turning their heads, they imprint me, taking a picture in their mind. Watching me closely they study to see if I have leadership skills, because respect is their number one rule. Once they respect you, they give you their whole heart and allegiance, investing in you with full loyalty. Guardians by nature they are devoted partners, and think of you as a teammate. They can be protective, and will place themselves in harms way to shield and defend you which makes them excellent in service or police work. They demand to be a part of your life, and will not be happy apart from you. Many people get German Shepherds, but are not ready for the responsibility of owning this breed. If you do not have the tools and skills to make a shepherd happy and content, it will lead to a confused dog, who as a working breed does not do well left to their own devises. If not given a job, they will create a job leading to disaster with the poor dog usually suffering the consequences.

Once again, we had a German Sheperd at the shelter separated from his owner. I walked to the front desk to find out why he was here. His paperwork stated he was picked up by animal control outside a bar tied to a table. When the owner of the bar was locking his doors at three in the morning he noticed the dog. He called animal control asking them to pick him up. It was noted on his paperwork his name is Bob, he's around seven years old, is microchipped and neutered. the owner was contacted by animal control, and told he could pick up his dog at the shelter, but first he would have to pay the fine, and get a release from them at the police station. Our staff had also contacted him, and he told them he would come in around ten to pick him up. Relieved, I went back to his kennel to take him out so he could go to the play yard and go to the bathroom. When I went back to his kennel he had not moved from his bed where I had seen him earlier.

"Hey Bob, you want to go outside? Your owner will be here soon to get you."

Watching him closely, I unlocked his kennel door. He got off his bed walking over to me with a nice tail wag, I placed the loose leash over his head so we could leave. As we walked through the dog runs he ignored all the barking dogs, staying close by my side. Reaching the outside door he sat down to wait for me.

"Good boy." I said, walking him out into the sunshine.

Entering the fenced enclosure, I took the lead off so he could walk around the yard. He smelled along the edges, and drank from the water bowl. Calling him back over he sat down beside me enjoying the warmth of the sun.

"You're a nice dog." I said, petting him.

The early morning was quiet and peaceful as we sat listening to the birds singing in the tree's surrounding us. Running my hand through the scruff on his neck, I knew I should take him back inside so I could start my day, but it was so nice to have a calm dog next to me. As we sat in the warmth of the new day, I was confident his owner would soon come to pick him up, and this will be the only time I would have with this dignified regal dog.

"What a lucky owner you have." I thought, putting the leash back on him so we could go inside.

I worked through the morning busy with other dogs, and did not have a chance to check on Bob. I assumed he had gone home, so when getting ready to leave at the end of the day I was surprised to see Bob's name still on the board.

"Hey!" I said, puzzled. "Didn't Bob's owner come in for him?"

Pat looked over at the dog board. "He never showed up."

Disgusted, I walked back to the kennels to get Bob out for a short time in the the play yard, sympathizing with him because of his owners lack of empathy. Coming back indoors, I left him in his kennel, and went to the front desk to call his owner. He did not answer the phone so I left a message for him to call us back as soon as possible.

I was off the next two days, and when I returned to work I was shocked to see Bob's name still on the board.

"What's going on with Bob's owner." I asked, Emmi.

"I have called him several times, and he always gives me the same excuse, saying he'll come in the next day, but he never shows up." She answered, frustrated.

Blowing out her breath, she continued. "the last time I tried calling I still did not reach him, so I left another message."

"Maybe we should go to the bar where he hangs out, and see if he's there, the jerk." I retorted.

We normally hold dogs for seventy two hours before they are evaluated, and put up for adoption. Because Bob's hold was up, I grabbed his paperwork to take back to my office so I could staple his evaluation on it once it was done. Grabbing a harness I walked back to the kennels to get Bob. He was quietly laying on his bed head down in his waiting position. I could hear dog dishes banging on the side of the sink in the kitchen as Kevin washed them.

"Good morning Kevin." I called out, standing at Bob's kennel door.

Hearing me he looked around the kitchen door.

"That is a supper nice dog." He said, giving me a good natured smile.

Waving the wash cloth at me, he continued. "I can't figure out why his owner hasn't come for him."

I felt irritated at the owner as I looked at Bob.

"Me either." I said, annoyed

Unlocking Bob's kennel I went in. He stood up with a full body stretch, and walked over to me sitting down. This time instead of only using a leash I slipped a harness over his head snapping the clasp in place. Clipping on the leash, I praised him for sitting quietly, and having such good manners.

"Okay, lets go outside." I told him.

Only then did he stand to walk beside me.

"See what I mean." Kevin said, still watching from the kitchen door.

"He is great to work with. I have walked him all weekend, and he seems perfect."

Leaving the dog runs Bob sat at each door waiting for me to move forward before stepping over the threshold. Outside he walked perfectly inches from my leg stopping when I stopped, moving forward when I stepped out.

"You are too good to be true." I said, Looking down at him.

He was so aware of my every move, and I began to wonder if he might be service trained. Curious, I walked him out to the parking lot towards the road as a car was turning in. He stopped, and sat waiting for the car to pass. We walked close to the dog runs where the dogs were barking, and jumping at the fence. He gently leaned on me to push me away from them. Now I was convinced he was trained for service, so I walked him towards the sidewalk where I had to step up on the sidewalk, he stopped not moving forward. Intrigued, I walked him under a tree with low hanging branches where he gently pulled me away from them. Back in my office I dropped a small towel on the floor.

"Pick up the towel Bob." I said, pointing at it.

Bob stood there looking at it, and then walked over to pick it up placing it on my lap. I was convinced now that Bob had some sort of service training so I wondered why his owner was not coming in for him? Could he not drive, and possibly be waiting for someone to bring him to the shelter? Why would he not tell us what was going on? I picked up the phone dialing his number, and he answered. I told him who I was, why I was calling, and if there was a problem with him coming in to get Bob?

"No, I just haven't had time." He said, in a gruff voice.

I told him his dog was off the seventy two hour hold, and if he did not pick him up in the next twenty four hours we would take applications on him starting the adoption process.

Annoyed, he responded. "I'll be in first thing in the morning."

Pausing, he continued. "Tell me something, can I get Bob back without a release from animal control?"

"That is out of our juristiction." I told him. "You must have a release to get your dog back."

Suspicious he had asked me that, I wondered what was really going on.

"I'll be there tomorrow." He ended the conversation slamming down the phone.

The next day came and went, without Bob's owner coming in for him.

Two days later as I walked to the front counter I noticed the animal control officer standing there.

"Officer Johnson." I said. "Bob, the German Shepherd you brought in is still here. We have been in contact with the owner at least four times, and he tells us he is coming each time, but never shows up."

He looked at me with a knowing shake of his head. "I was just talking to Emmi about him."

"I can't understand it" I replied. "The dog seems to be service trained."

Shrugging his shoulders, he looked at us. "He is service trained, but his owner will not be in."

Now he had our full attention, and we looked at him surprised.

"Bob's owner is a felon, and the police have a warrant out on him." He continued. "He's afraid to come into the police station to get the release on his dog."

He picked up his paperwork to leave. "Adopt him out." He said. "This dog deserves a better home."

Waving the papers at us, he continued. "It's a matter of time before they catch this guy, so Bob would end up here anyway."

Looking in the office door of our director, he asked. "I do have one request though, when you adopt Bob out, place him out of county."

He picked up a pen signing the release on him. Walking towards the door to leave, he turned. "I have another request, please tell his new owner to change his name, it would be best for everyone."

We were all relieved Bob was released to us, and now we could adopt him out. I picked up the release looking at it, and knew the first person I was going to talk with about him.

Kerrie came in every Saturday as a volunteer helper. She had been coming to the shelter for at least five years to oversee a young man who helped us clean. She is an animal lover, filling her home with cats and dogs. Her preferred breed of dog, the German Shepherd. At one point she had three shepherds living in her home, and if there was a need, she would take fosters from a Shepherd Rescue. Because of this, she knew other people who loved the German Shepherd breed. Two of her shepherds had died from old age, and now she was down to one. Her remaining dog was getting older, and it would not be long before she would have to say another sad goodby. If you could rate love and care given to dogs, she was an all time high. They were the love of her life, pampered and adored. She watched the dog board closely, and if she noticed a German Shepherd on the board she eagerly asked us about them. On Saturday morning, when Kerrie came in, I brought Bob up front to meet her. She was delighted, and called him over to sweet talk him while she pet him. He sat next to her leaning against her leg enjoying the attention she gave him while she gently stroked his coat. I told her he was service trained, and even though I could not give details about why he was with us he needed to be placed outside of our county, and renamed. I asked her if she knew of any shepherd people in need of a service dog. She looked at me for a moment contemplating, and then burst out.

"My mom!"

Smiling, she said. "She lives alone, and her house is outside of town on five acres. She even lives out of county on one of the islands."

She sat there quiet for a moment. "I have been more concerned about her lately since she is by herself, and getting older. She is very independent and self sufficient, but I think the companionship of a dog would be wonderful for her."

Looking down at Bob, she continued. "He would be perfect because of his service training, mom is now in her seventies, and I think she would enjoy his company."

Looking at Kerrie, I asked. "Does your mom understand this breed?"

She rolled her eyes. "Where do you think I get my love for German Shepherds, we always had shepherds while I was growing up."

She took her phone out of her pocket. "Let me call her, and see what she thinks."

While she called, I went to get a application so she could take it to her mom. I hoped this was our answer for Bob. Later in the morning when the director came in, I told her about Kerrie's mom, asking her if she would approve her application.

"Let's do it," She said with a smile. "This would be a great home, and a solution to our concerns in this case."

Kerrie, called the shelter later in the day telling Emmi her mom was interested. They came the next day to meet Bob, but when they arrived they had only a few minutes to get acquainted, because he was scheduled to go to the vet, for a well check, and get his rabies vaccine. Determined, they came back the next day to spend more time with him. They both recognized he was a very special dog, and I think Bob knew they were special people. He leaned close to Kerrie's mom, throwing his head back to admire her. After spending time with him Karri's mom told the staff she was interested in taking him home. Emmi told her she was approved, so they did the paperwork with Bob renamed Nox. We knew Nox was going to a wonderful home where he could continue his job with a new person. He would devote his life to her, and she would give him the best care a dog could have.

On the Saturday's, after Nox was adopted, Kerrie was always excited to tell me his many adventures, and his adjustments to his new home. As she told me these stories I began to see things from Nox's perspective, and point of view. He left with a woman he did not know, but she was kind, and he would take his time to study her so he could learn how to best serve her. He had always been the co-pilot in the car, so naturally when he saw the empty seat beside her, he jumped into it. This was not allowed, and he was immediately put into the back seat. Now it is really hard for a co-pilot to help navigate a car from the back seat so he made a second attempt, but again was placed in the back seat as a passenger, this time he stayed. He knew he was going to have to train her in this area, and he would wait her out. When he got to the house it was big with a lot of space, the food was good, and she had made up a nice comfy bed beside her bed which was very adequate, especially because it was his job to sleep beside her at night. There were several cats in the home, and he could tolerate them, but the deer that came from the meadow into the yard could not be tolerated. So he drew a fine line close to the edge of the meadow, and began to teach them not to cross it. It was a lot of work to protect this new charge of his, because she was so independent. He worried about hazards that may endanger her, especially when she declined his help. She obviously thought of Nox as her charge so he was going to have to persuade her the rolls had been reversed, and he had a job to do. She introduced him to the island and the town, and even from the backseat he was learning his way around as he enjoyed the rides in the car. He took up his post next to her while she had coffee with friends, or laid quietly beside her while she was having her hair done. Soon, she decided to pamper him with a day at the spa having him bathed, and his toe nails clipped. He took this with good humor enjoying himself, but soon discovered this was going to be a frequent event. Sometimes she would leave him there to play with other dogs, or go on long hikes. He did enjoy this, but was very relieved to come back home to make sure she was safe, and make sure those pesky deer had honored his boundary lines. As the summer days began to grow hot, she decided not to take him because of the heat. He could not understand why she did not put his harness on, because once he was harnessed he was allowed to go anywhere with her. Left alone at home, he climbed the stairs to the landing where a huge window was. There he laid to wait, and watch the driveway for her car. When he saw her coming home he ran down the stairs to greet her at the front door so he could go back to work.

It seemed to him she did not comprehend what he was trained to do, but as the summer progressed she let him take more of a role as her trusted guardian. He laid in the shade of a tree watching as she mowed, or while she worked on her many projects around the yard. When autumn arrived, and the temperatures cooled. The leaves began falling to the ground, and she spent long hours outside raking preparing her yard for the fast approaching winter. One afternoon as Nox was at his post watching her, she tripped over a rake which was hidden by the fallen leaves. Laying on the ground she struggled to get up. Nox ran over standing close to her so she could lean against him to lift herself up. I think it was at this point in their relationship she began to understand who Nox was, and as her companion she needed to trust him to do his job. Weeks went to months, and months to years. Nox and his charge became a happy companionable unit, a team. Nox loved his new person he was reassigned too, carrying out what he was trained to do. They happily resided together filling their days with long walks, evening fires, and a companionship that lodged in both their hearts. She trusted him, and he devoted himself to her as they enjoyed each others company becoming trusted friends.

When I called Kerrie to tell her I was writing about Nox she started to cry. She told me Nox had died peacefully in her mother's arms. He had loved her completely as she had loved him, calling him her miracle dog. It must have been hard for him to leave her, after all he still had a job to do. If you think about it, service dogs are miracles, and give heart and soul to their person, making life easier for them. They make possible the things in life that are not possible even if it is just companionship. They are outstanding dogs, an example of what a canine is capable of doing. Serving people brings joy to their hearts, and it is the purist form of love a dog can give to help mankind. Nox and his owner experienced this, they were true friends. He gave her his full loyalty love and commitment, and she gave him her complete love, allowing him to become the co-pilot of her life.

"A dog is the only thing on earth that loves you more than he loves himself."

JOSH BILLINGS

DIETER

We all stood looking out of the shelter window, wrinkling our noses as it continued to pour down rain. Not only was it raining, but it was a deluge, coming down in heavy sheets, impeding our sight from seeing the main road.

"I hate the rain," Pat said, standing there fidgeting. "I don't know why I live here."

I knew why I lived here. Where else could you have the ocean and mountains with all of their natural beauty? Living in a farming community spared us the clamor and chaos of the city. If we wanted to go there, we were only an hour away, but here it was peaceful and calm—a good place to put down roots.

We were waiting for the Tacoma shelter van to drive into our shelter parking lot so we could exchange dogs. We had four dogs who had been with us for over three months. At the moment, they had no prospects for adoption, so Tacoma agreed to take them, and in exchange, they were bringing us four of their residents, who had been with them for a while. In the shelter world, we have a motto of "fresh eyes," and most of the time, it works. As I stood at my post listening to the dogs chewing on bully sticks or comfortably sleeping in their crates behind me, I couldn't help thinking about what their new life would be like living in the city. In ways, I felt I was betraying them by sending them to the noisy suburbs, but if this gave them a chance of adoption, it was a win for them.

Suddenly, through the downpour, we could see the dim lights from a van turning into our parking lot. We pulled on our raincoats and stepped out into the torrential rain as the staff members of Tacoma slid the van door open. Carrying the crates in, we placed them on the floor and then helped transfer our dogs out to their van. A Tacoma staff member handed us the new dogs' records, her long hair dripping water onto the paperwork. We waved them off as she ran, splashing through the water to the dryness of her van.

After they drove off, we turned to look at the kennels sitting on the floor. One in particular, a medium-sized crate, was in full motion, jumping and bouncing across the linoleum. I walked over to look down at the placard which read Dieter. Bending over, I looked in. There, looking out at me, was a Parson Jack Russell Terrier. She was panting from all of her exertion, and I could tell she was a ball of energy. Reaching down, I opened the door as she shot out like a rocket, running through and around our legs. She ran over to the desk cabinets, jumping perpendicularly up onto the countertop. There she indignantly proceeded to bark at us, yapping her unhappiness at this unnecessary journey and now experiencing all these strange people who were staring at her.

"Oh, oh!" said Pat. "We have a live one."

I walked over to the cabinet and carefully reached out my hand. "Hello, Dieter."

Recognizing her name, she wagged her stub tail but continued to yap, yap, yap at us. She was a beautiful little thing, mostly white with a few brown spots. She had the usual pricked ears with the tips flapped forward, giving her an inquisitive look. Both ears were sable brown, with the same color running down to circle each snapping black eye. There was a blaze of white running down the middle of her forehead between each eye, which continued down over her muzzle, showing off her black nose. Sturdy legs supported her stiff little body, ready for movement, and bouncing on her front feet, she waved her stub tail like a flag pointed towards the ceiling. I pulled her paperwork out of the packet to read it.

"It says here that her family gave her up because she killed a goat," I read out loud, surprised.

We all reacted in amazement as we looked at this little dog standing on our counter, barking loudly.

"How does a little dog like that kill a goat?" Pat said, waving her hand at Dieter.

"I don't know!" I answered. "Maybe it was a tiny goat. They are a working breed that will hunt and kill rats."

By now, Dieter had stopped barking and had pushed her hindquarters back, laying down to watch us.

"Well, whatever the case, we need to get her off my front counter and get these dogs in their kennels so they can settle in," our director instructed.

Her directive turned our thoughts to the importance of the moment, so the staff hustled about to get the dogs out of their kennels. I scooped Dieter off the counter, put a leash on her, and walked her to her new kennel where she would be staying.

We soon learned Dieter hated the kennel environment. She jumped up and down, barking, begging for attention from anyone who walked by. This had the opposite effect on people who hurried away, not showing interest in her, thinking she barked all the time and might have too much energy for them. Her constant barking was unsettling to the other dogs in the surrounding kennels, and soon we had a pod of barking dogs. I knew she was showing a lot of stress, so I started bringing her into my office when I could. It was a quiet place for her to be, where she could play, chew on her toys, or take a nap.

I wondered how she would be in a home environment, so I brought her home in the evenings. I hoped that being in my home, she would relax and become more presentable at the shelter during the day. The first week went well, as she played with my older dog. She went for evening walks with us and took control over the couch, stretching out to take long naps.

After a couple of days in our home, she focused on my old senior kitty. If my cat came into the living room, Dieter would watch her from her prominent position on the couch and wait for her to reach the center of the room. Then she would make a flying leap off the couch to chase her. My cat would scramble away in fear, trying to find a hiding place beneath chairs or a bed. Dieter, in full tracking mode, would circle her hiding place, making a huffing noise, unnerving my poor kitty. My poor cat, who had never feared dogs, was now being haunted, and Dieter was the hunter. The evening she coaxed my older dog into the chase, I knew she had lost her privilege of coming home with me, and once again, she would have to spend nights in my office at the shelter.

A couple of weeks went by with her housed in my office. Then, a man came through the shelter doors and walked to the front desk. I was behind the desk working on some paperwork when he spoke.

"Excuse me," he said. "My name is Paul Anderson. Would you be so kind as to direct me to where I could view the dogs?"

I looked up to see an older man with a kind, sad smile. His eyes were red-rimmed behind his glasses hanging off the edge of his nose, and his cheeks bore a non-caring shade of grey stubble. His shirt and pants were clean, well-tailored, but rumpled, and I could tell someone had once lovingly ironed them.

In a muffled voice, he said, "My wife died three months ago, and I can't stand the quietness in my home any longer. As I drank my tea this morning, I started thinking a dog might help to fill the empty space and give a lonely old man some company."

Fidgeting with his hands where he still wore his wedding ring, he continued, "What do you think? Would a dog be a good companion for a lonely old man?"

"Yes, Mr. Anderson," I said, looking up at him. "I think a dog would be a wonderful companion for you."

He smiled. "I walk every day and am fairly active. Do you have one in mind?"

"Do you have cats?" I asked.

"No, no, don't care for cats," he replied.

"Well then, I may have just the dog for you, and she's just as lonely as you are."

I took him to my office, introducing him to Dieter, hoping she would work her magic on him. I left, shutting the door behind me, and stood outside listening, thinking this might be a perfect match. With Dieter's high-spirited joy and playfulness, I soon heard laughter coming from the other side of the door. I walked down the hall to give them some time to get acquainted. On returning, Paul was sitting on a chair, holding Dieter in his lap.

"I think we could be wonderful friends. What do you think?"

"Yes," I replied. "I think it's possible."

Excited, the staff prepared all the paperwork, making it official that Dieter would go home to live with Paul. As they drove away, Dieter was sitting in Paul's lap, panting. We waved, sending them good wishes for a happy life together.

Two days after the adoption, Paul called the shelter with the dreaded news he was going to have to bring Dieter back.

"I can't keep her," he murmured. "On our walk yesterday, she tried to attack another dog. We were on a walking trail when a man with a large dog came around the corner, and she tried to attack it. She leaves small dogs alone, but this was a large dog— a big pit bull. I am so afraid she is going to get hurt or killed acting the way she does." There was a pause, and then he broke down, saying, "I'm so sorry, but I can't stand the thought of it."

We told him he could bring her back, and on the following morning, a broken-hearted Paul brought Dieter back to the shelter. When he left, he looked more rumpled than ever, petting Dieter on her head as he sobbed. Poor little Dieter. Once again she found herself confined to my office, where she curled up on her bed. I was worried about who would take this feisty Jack Russell home.

The weekend went by, and early Monday morning, we received a phone call from Paul. "Is Dieter still there?" he asked, anxiety in his voice.

"Yes, she's still here," Emmi answered him.

The phone was silent for a moment. Then he said, in a pleading voice, "I miss her. Could I have her back? I have thought all weekend and have made a plan to keep her safe."

He caught his breath. "It is so quiet and lonely here."

He waited for Emmi's response, but before she could answer, he implored, "Please! I would love to have her back."

With relief, Emmi told him to come and get his dog. Two hours later, Paul came for Dieter, and this time, it was for good. Paul called once a year to tell us how Dieter was, sharing stories of her funny antics and the joy she had brought to his lonely home. Ending the conversation, he would again thank us for Dieter.

As time goes by, the dogs who have made an impression become a faded sweet memory we revisit with a smile. When Paul called one morning with sad news of Dieter's passing from cancer, we were all very sad for him and could hear the sorrow and grief in his voice.

"They were seven wonderful years I had with her."

"We are so sorry," I said. "Dieter was a very special dog and a good friend to you."

"Yes, I loved her so much. I think in time I may want to get another dog." He paused. "I know I can't replace her, but I would like it to be a Jack Russell."

"I will watch for you," I replied.

"I am so sorry, I am crying," he sobbed. "I loved her so much."

I hung up the phone, feeling sorry for him. Looking through my desk drawer, I found Dieter's picture and taped it to the front of my computer as a reminder to watch for another dog for Paul.

Four months went by without a Jack Russell coming into the shelter. Then, on a bright spring morning, I came to work to see a Jack Russell Terrier written on the board.

"When did she come in?" I asked Emmi.

"She came in over the weekend. Her owner died, and the family does not want her because she's an older dog."

"Where is she?" I asked.

"She's in kennel seven," she said sadly. "I feel so bad for her, poor thing."

I walked to kennel seven. Looking in, I could see a Jack Russell curled in a tight ball on her bed. I whispered to her, and she gazed up at me with sad eyes looking out of a grey senior face. When she did not recognize me, she laid her head back down, giving an unhappy sigh. She closed her depressed eyes, hoping these new unfamiliar surroundings would disappear, and she would be back home again.

I unlocked her kennel door, stepping in. "Hey, little girl."

Kneeling down, I talked to her, trying to assure and comfort her. Coaxing her off her bed, she walked over to me with a slow, gentle wag of her tail. Her tags on her collar jingled as I reached down to pet her. Turning the heart-shaped tag over, it read "Jelly Bean."

"Jelly Bean!" That is a wonderful name for you, my friend."

I put a leash on her so I could take her out of her kennel to go for a walk outdoors. When I brought her back to my office, I sat on the floor, petting her. As I sat there, I found myself drawn to Dieter's picture taped to my computer, which reminded me of Paul.

Hugging Jelly Bean, I said, "I have to make a phone call."

Hoping Paul was ready, I made the call, telling him about Jelly Bean. There was a long silence before he spoke.

"I still miss Dieter terribly, and I'm not sure if I am ready for another dog."

I clutched the phone, waiting for him to speak again.

"Let me think about it. I may come to meet her sometime this coming week."

Two days later, Paul walked into the shelter to meet our sad little Jelly Bean. Emmi took him into one of the adoption rooms, leaving to get her. Excited, she came to my office, telling me Paul was here, and she had left him with Jelly Bean to get acquainted. When I stepped in to greet Paul, Jelly Bean was lying on his lap as he gently petted the top of her head.

"I think she needs me," he said, looking up at me.

"Yes, she does," I smiled back at them.

"I know she is old, but so am I. That is the cruelty of life: we all get old. I think Jelly Bean and I can do it together, don't you?"

"I certainly do," I said.

After completing the paperwork, we once again sent Paul home with a companion dog and friend. Two elderly beings who needed each other and would help each other through a time of sorrow and loss. These two would fill the void in each other's hearts.

Waving from the door, Emmi said, "There is no better therapy in this world than a man with his dog."

Smiling, I replied, "Or a dog with her man."

"Dog's are not our whole life, but they make our life whole."

ROGER A. CARAS

MURPHY

Murphy's law is the belief that if anything could go wrong, it probably will, and it was ironic when a dog came to the shelter named Murphy, because this law seemed to apply. The owners brought him to the shelter, stating he had too much energy for them. Murphy, a Border Collie-Lab mix, waved them off with a non-caring attitude, looking for the next adventure in his life. He was a beautiful dog with a long white coat and patches of black. If you could get eye contact, you could see his brown intelligent eyes. His black ears pricked forward as if pointing to his next adventure. He seemed to have a happy, carefree manner. Looking at every situation as an opportunity to use his clever and ingenious mind. He soon became a favorite of the staff and volunteers, but had a way of creating chaos or getting himself into some sort of predicament. He could get every dog barking and raising a hullabaloo as he happily walked by their kennels. Outside, he would get his collar caught in the fence or the leash wrapped around his legs, and sometimes it would take two staff members and a volunteer to free him. It never seemed to phase him when he was in an unpleasant situation, for in his mind everything was an adventure, even being caught in a fence.

His evaluation went well, and our director thought he would do well in an active family home. Off went Murphy, only to be returned in less than three days because of chewing up the children's toys and incessantly barking when they put him in the garage at night. Their neighbors called complaining, and instead of putting Murphy in the house with them, they brought him back, telling us he was too disruptive. Once back at the shelter, more mayhem happened with Murphy once again getting himself into trouble. We always have new staff being trained, and they are told to never put feather comforters into kennels with dogs. Before the donation barrel had been gone through one day, a new staff member grabbed a comforter and laid it neatly on Murphy's bed. Later in the morning, a visitor came to the front desk with feathers clinging to her clothing and in her hair.

"I just came out of the dog runs," she said. "And in the last pod, there are feathers everywhere."

"Oh, shit," Pat said.

We all ran to the dog kennel area, stopping to look in the window of Pod F. There, floating through the air, were white feathers—millions of them—and they were everywhere. It looked like it had been snowing, with most of the feathers floating in Murphy's kennel. He sat on his bed amongst the piles of feathery down clinging to his coat, and with a look of guiltless innocence, he was not about to take the blame for this carnage.

He looked at us as if to say, "It wasn't me!"

The evidence was there surrounding him, with one feather laying neatly across the top of his nose. It took us hours to clean the dog run up as feathers floated everywhere. We were still finding feathers months later, when out of nowhere, a small white feather would drift down and gently glide to the floor.

After that escapade, our director once again picked a home for Murphy. This time, he went with an active young couple without children. They were hikers, kayakers, and campers, spending most of their free time exploring the Northwest. We all thought this would be a great outcome for Murphy. The family brought Murphy back after only a month in this home. On the day they returned him to the shelter, they said they could not keep him at home. They explained that when they were away or at work, he would find ingenious ways to leave the house. Once out, he would escape to visit the neighbors to play with their dog or children. He was great as long as they were home, but the minute they left, he would start his remodeling project to get out. So far, they had replaced the window of the front door, the door into the garage, and screens to windows. The last weekend he was with them, they put him into his kennel to go on a date and get a quick cup of coffee. While they were sitting outside of the coffee shop enjoying their coffee in the morning sun, Murphy trotted by with another dog. They could not believe it, and pointing at him, the woman said, "Is that Murphy?"

"I think it is," her husband responded.

They tried to call him over, but in a nonchalant and carefree way, Murphy continued on with the other dog as if he did not know them and did not have a worry in the world.

They spent the rest of the morning searching the neighborhood for him. Eventually, they gave up and returned home. As they pulled up to their garage, they noticed Murphy sitting on the front steps of their neighbor's house with the little neighbor boy. Both were smiling as they waited patiently for them. In the house, they found the kennel intact, but the gate pulled inward, and a fresh tear in the window screen gave him access to the outside world. Now they were frightened he would get hit by a car or hurt in one of his escapades across town.

"We think he needs a family with children," they told us.

Back at the shelter, Murphy was once again happily causing chaos and random calamities. Out of boredom, he started lifting the caps on the drains in his kennel to bury his toys. The toys would disappear into the deep recesses of the drainfield, causing it to plug up, backing up the septic system. Now we had to cover the front of poor Murphy's kennel with signs stating, "No comforters or toys."

This made us look like a jackass because we would not allow this poor dog to have toys or a nice, comfortable blanket. We all loved Murphy, but our feelings were running thin with the pandemonium that seemed to follow him. Murphy, by now, had been with us off and on for about two months, and we knew he was going to require a very special home.

Some days at the shelter are so busy they would call me to the front to help answer the phones. On one of those days, I answered the phone to hear a slurred voice blurt out, "This is Phhhil."

"Good morning, Phil. How can I help you?"

"I'm cooming to get Murrrphhy," he said in a garbled voice.

I could tell this man was very drunk and most likely not able to drive, so I asked him politely, "Well, that would be great. When can we expect you?"

"When I geet therre," he mumbled back at me.

"Okay, great!" I said. "We'll see you when you get here."

Hanging up the phone, I started laughing and turned to see Emmi and Pat looking at me with curious looks.

"Who was that?" asked Emmi.

"Oh, some drunk guy who told me he was coming to get Murphy."

"Oh, great. Just what we need," Pat said, waving her arms in the air.

"Well, he won't make it," I said thoughtfully. "He's too drunk to drive."

The drunk man became an afterthought as we continued with our busy day. A couple of hours later, Emmi looked into my office, and in a whisper, she said, "He's here."

"Who's here?" I said.

Pausing, she blurted out, "That drunk guy you talked with on the phone. He's at the front desk."

"What? How did he get here?" I said, standing up.

"Well, he must have driven a car," she said while motioning for me to come to the front desk. I walked up front to see a tall, gaunt man in his late sixties. He appeared rumpled from head to toe, with his shirt buttoned askew. His eyes were red-rimmed and creased, his chin and jawline covered in stubble. In his hands, he held a cap he twisted as he stood there swaying back and forth, trying to keep his balance.

"Are you Phil?" I asked in surprise.

"You mustt be the laady I talked withhh thhis morning," he hiccuped.

"Yes, my name is Julie," I said, shaking his hand. "Can I ask you something? Did you drive here?"

My imagination was seeing visions of him swerving his way toward the shelter in a car.

"Nooope, I don't drrive," he hiccuped. "I have a deesignater driiver," he said, pointing towards the door.

I looked to where he was pointing as a man walked toward me, introducing himself as Bob, Phil's friend and designated driver. On his head, he wore a cap with the wording Vietnam War Veteran. Then the pieces fell into place. I quietly introduced myself to Bob, asking, "Is Phil a Vietnam vet?"

He sadly shook his head yes, and I turned, looking at Phil, feeling the sorrow and despondency of what had happened to our young men and women from the Vietnam era.

The Vietnam War, our politicians claimed, was a war to prevent communism. With America being the big brother and guardian of the world, they offered our most precious commodity: our young men and women. They sent these young people to Vietnam when they were as young as eighteen. Our youth and future, who only wanted to go to college, have friends, and live their lives with new and exciting experiences—but not war. They did not want the experience of being on a battlefield, watching their comrades wounded or die. Every night, as we watched the nightly news, we would see a line run across the bottom of our television screen telling us how many of our men or women died that day. It could range from two or three, and on one particular day, two hundred and forty-six.

Finally, after eleven years of fighting, with 58,000 American men and women dying, and 150,000 Americans wounded, our remaining boys and women returned home. It did not stop communism, but it made some Americans very wealthy. The rich filled their pockets and banks with money, while we stood at open graves watching the earth swallow up our loved ones. It left a horrible scar and distrust of our government on the minds of the American people. We watched our youth returning home old beyond their years, not able to cope with the images and memories that scarred their minds. With no help from the government, they self-medicated with drugs and alcohol. I questioned Bob further, asking him about Phil's living conditions and how responsible he would be with a dog. He assured me Phil always had a dog and had taken good care of them. Phil had recently lost his dog to old age, and having a dog around helped him cope better. He told me other vets like himself were always available for Phil or other vets who did not cope well after the war.

"We have a close bond and a brotherhood to look after each other. Phil," he said, "is one of the special ones. He needs extra care. He just saw too much," he said, sorrow in his eyes.

The girls were all up front watching this tall man drunkenly swaying, trying to push the horrible memories away.

Looking at them, I said, "I'm going to handle this. Please get Murphy."

I took Phil and Bob to my office, telling them one of the staff members would be in shortly with Murphy, and they could visit with him. Later, I went back in and could see Murphy had happily made up with them, showing off his lighthearted mannerism. He joyfully ran around the room, happy to be free of the confines of a kennel. I explained to them he was a free spirit and undisciplined, but he loved people. They both smiled as I handed Phil an adoption application. Bob helped him fill it out, and I took the application to our director, ready to go to war for this veteran who needed a dog—and for Murphy, who needed a veteran.

When I laid the application down in front of her, I could tell she had overheard the girls talking. She sat there, thumbing through the application, shaking her head.

"Murphy needs this guy," I told her. "He is home all the time nursing his wounds through a bottle, but he has a lot of help from his veteran friends."

She looked at me a little apprehensively, so I continued talking, trying to convince her of the need this man and this dog had for each other.

"He needs to laugh, and Murphy can make him laugh," I said.

"How is he going to cope with Murphy when he tears something up or runs away?"

"He isn't worried about fixing things around the house. He can't even heal his broken heart," I replied.

Picking up the application, she looked at it once again.

"All right then, I trust your opinion on this," she said thoughtfully. "Hopefully, Murphy won't have to be returned to us again, and I sincerely wish this poor man the best," she said in a thoughtful tone.

Picking up her pen, she wrote "Approved" in big red letters.

Murphy went home that day, and I did not see or hear anything about him for three years. Then, late one summer evening, as my husband and I drove through a small town, we saw a man walking down the road with his dog.

"Stop the car," I demanded.

Getting out, I walked up to Phil and looked down at Murphy, who sat down beside him, wagging his tail.

"Phil, do you remember me?" I said, reaching out my hand.

"Surre, you'rre the laady from the shhhelter," he slurred, shaking my hand. "Murrrphy, do you rememberrr thish nice laady?"

Murphy sat there, flicking his tail and stirring up the dust.

"Shake herr haand, Murrrph," he said, as Murphy raised his paw.

"He hash been the beest dog. He waalks to the taaverrn everry night withh mee and sitss underr the stool until I'mm ready too go hoome," he said, swaying. "He's faithful, my Murrph is."

"I'm glad," I said. "Murphy has a nice home with you."

"Yup, he ish a faithfulll frriend, my Murrph," he mumbled, patting Murphy on the head.

"Well, bye, Phil. You take good care of yourself," I said, shaking his hand for the last time. Leaning down, I looked into Murphy's eyes. "And Murphy, you take good care of our veteran."

When I got back in the car, my husband questioned me. "Who was that?"

Looking back, I said, "That is a Vietnam vet friend of mine with his dog, Murphy."

As we drove away, I said, "You know Murphy's law?"

"Uh-huh," he replied. "It is the belief that if anything can go wrong, it will."

"Well, in this case," I said, "Murphy's law doesn't apply. This Murphy made a man's life much, much better."

Still looking back, I watched Phil teeter and wobble down

the road with his friend Murphy, who walked happily beside him.

"Dogs have a way of finding the people who need them."

THOM JONES

ZORO

Some dogs steal your heart the minute you meet them, as Zorro did mine. On a cold evening in January, I was walking through the shelter, making a last-minute check on the dogs. I shivered as I felt the cold from the outdoors penetrating the hallways, knowing we would wake up to snow the next day.

I walked into the small dog area and noticed a little dog's white rear end with a docked tail sticking out from beneath a quivering blanket as he tried to stay warm.

"Are you cold?" I said, looking through the glass at him.

To my surprise, out popped a black head with snappy, expressive eyes peering at me. Crawling from under his blanket, he stretched with a full bow, and trotted over to me. He was a Fox Terrier, and I had never seen a dog with his coloration before. He had a smooth white coat, and aside from his black head, there was one tiny black mark next to his docked tail, which stuck straight up into the air, pointing at the ceiling. His black head had an elongated nose and ears that were pricked forward, folding at the center with the tips pointing down. His front and back legs were stiff and straight, making him look as though he was standing on his tiptoes.

He twisted his head back and forth and waved his stubby tail with a good-natured friendliness at my appearance. Making a quick spin, he barked, trying to keep my attention. As he whirled around, I couldn't take my eyes off his back. Opening the door, I stopped him in mid-spin and turned him around so I could look more closely.

Most of the hair was missing on the top of his back, with sores that were raw and oozing. A few of the wounds had dried and had a yellow crust formed around the scabs. When I touched them, he whined, trying to wiggle away from me, but remained a good sport about being handled. I gently draped his blanket over him and picked him up so I could carry him to my director's office. Knocking on her door, I stepped in.

"Is this the new guy?" she said, looking up.

"Yes," I said, pulling the blanket away from his back so she could see it.

"The girls told me about him, so I scheduled an appointment for him tomorrow to see the vet and have a skin scrape done. Once we know what this is, we can start medicating him." She got up from her desk and pulled her glasses down her nose to look closely at his back. "Oh, that is nasty, isn't it?" she said, wrinkling her nose as she gently ran her hand over his back.

"The person who brought him in said it wasn't her dog, but I wonder," she queried. "They may have been the owners and were using home remedies instead of taking him to a vet."

She rubbed his ears, baby-talking to him. "You are so cute! Yes, you are."

Straightening up, she said in a serious voice, "Make sure you wash your hands because we don't know what we are dealing with. We did black-light him for ringworm, and it was negative, but whatever this is, it might be contagious." Walking back around her desk, she reached down and picked up a half-eaten apple, taking a bite.

"Poor little dog," she said, chewing.

Smiling, I carefully wrapped him in his blanket and walked back to the small dog area. His tail was wagging against my side, keeping the beat of my steps. Placing him back in his kennel, I fluffed out his bed, making a deep crevasse for him to nestle into. As I covered him with an extra blanket, he cuddled in, looking back at me, warm and cozy.

"Good night, my friend," I said. "I will see you in the morning." I turned to leave, shutting off the lights for the night.

The next morning, waking up to about six inches of snow didn't surprise me. It was beautiful outdoors, looking like a winter wonderland; the branches of the laden trees hung low, with the lower limbs touching the ground. I put on extra layers, dreading the drive on the icy roads because people in the Northwest hate to drive in the snow. When I pulled into the shelter parking lot, I could see most of the staff had not yet arrived. Wading through the deep snow to the front door, I hoped they would try, since the animals depended on them.

It was toasty warm as I entered the lobby, stomping the snow off my boots and removing my coat. I walked back to the small dog area to check on the little dog from the night before. When I turned on the light, he peered out at me from under the blankets, but he did not get up.

"It is cold this morning, my friend," I told him. "Stay where you are and stay warm."

I could hear the muted conversations at the front desk and knew staff were arriving, ready to start their day. Turning the lights off, I walked back up front, hearing Pat complaining to the staff about the cold and the terrible drivers she had encountered on her way to work. She was extra cranky this morning, ordering people to clean up the melting snow they had trailed in.

While we were chatting around the desk, our focus shifted to the window when headlights appeared in the parking lot. We watched our director trying to make a run for the front door, spinning the wheels on her car. The car zigzagged back and forth as she revved up the motor, only making it halfway before she had to stop. Getting out of her car, she labored through the heavy snow toward the front door.

When she walked in, we laughed at her comical attire as she shook the snow off her jacket and looked at us from beneath her hat. She must have dug through her husband's belongings, trying to find the warmest winter clothes. She pulled her hat firmly down over her head, making her look like a formidable Russian commander in his fur-lined trooper hat. With the furry bill snapped to the top and the furry ear flaps strapped tight under her chin, her teeth chattered from the cold as she instructed us on how the day would go.

"We will not open today," she said, pulling the hat off her head. "Once the cleaning is done, I am sending most of you home."

"I will stay," Emmi said. "I'll call to reschedule the vet appointment for the new dog."

"Yes, I doubt the vet clinic will be open today, so it looks like we will have to wait until tomorrow when the roads are plowed," commented our director. "Hopefully, we will have better roads in the morning."

It was disappointing the little dog would have to wait to be checked out by a vet. We knew he needed vet care, and the only thing holding it up was this miserable weather. Hopefully, the storm would let up in the next couple of days, making it safer to drive on the roads. I stayed at the shelter with Emmi and the director for the rest of the day.

Late in the afternoon, after we had medicated, given second feedings, and tucked everyone in for the night, we got ready to leave. It was snowing again, with big flakes drifting down, piling on top of what had already accumulated during the day. We were putting our coats on when Emmi noticed headlights pulling onto the shelter drive. A pickup truck plowed its way to the front door, sliding to a stop. The door opened, and out stepped our favorite vet.

Our director opened the front door for him. "Dr. Vincent, what are you doing out in this terrible weather?"

"You called yesterday about a dog with skin problems," he answered. "I'm on my way home, so I thought I would take a chance someone was still here."

We led him back to the small dog area, and as we entered the room, the little dog stood up to greet us, wagging his stubby tail. Emmi opened the door to his kennel, calling him over while the vet put on his glasses.

"Poor little guy, what a mess you are," he said as he gently felt around his back.

He dug into his coat pocket, pulling out everything he would need to take a skin scrape. He scraped several places, putting them on slides and placing another slide over the top. Slipping them into a small plastic bag, he sealed it and put it back into his coat pocket. The little dog never fussed with all the handling; he seemed to know Dr. Vincent was trying to help him.

"I will look at them under the microscope when I get home and call you tomorrow with the results. Then we can make a plan on how to help this little guy," he said, gently petting the little dog and rubbing his ears with his fingers.

"He is really cute; what are you naming him?"

Thoughtfully, I said, "I was thinking about calling him Zorro."

Laughing, Dr. Vincent said, "Well, it fits him because he looks like he is wearing a mask. You know Zorro in Spanish means fox, and he is a Fox Terrier."

Smiling, our director said, "Well, he is charming; we may have to get him a black cape to match his mask."

We all laughed as Dr. Vincent listened to his heart, checked his mouth, and looked in his ears. "Well, except for his back, he seems to be in good health." With a last pat on his head, he tucked him under the blankets. "Good night, little Zorro."

We turned the lights out and walked with him to the front door. Looking outside, we could see the wind had picked up, pushing the new snow around and making small drifts.

"Thank you for coming out in this weather," our director said. "We appreciate all you do for the shelter."

Pulling his hat down over his ears, Dr. Vincent smiled. "You all be careful driving home; it is really icy, and the roads are bad."

Waving, he ran for the warmth of his pickup. As we stood together watching him leave, little did we know our champion vet would have a hard time curing this little dog. As for the cape, it would be replaced by a onesie.

Dr. Vincent called first thing in the morning to let us know Zorro had demodicosis, or demodectic mange, caused by mites. Because of the lack of treatment, his open sores resulted in a severe infection. He told us he would bring over some ointment, and a medicated shampoo to bathe him with. He also wanted us to start him on antibiotics to stop the infection.

"It is not contagious to humans," he said. "I don't want you or your staff to worry you could get it from him."

True to his word, he came late in the afternoon to deliver everything Zorro would need to get better. Kevin cleaned out his kennel, putting in a new bed with clean blankets while I lathered him in the medicated shampoo, giving him his first bath. Once he was dry, I smoothed on the ointment, covering all his sores. Zorro loved the attention, burying himself in the towels and zooming around the room. We laughed at all his antics while he amused us with his playful romps, running, and happy whirls.

"Okay, El Zorro," I laughed, trying to catch him.

Kevin chuckled as he watched him. "He already acts like he is feeling better."

He picked Zorro up, tucking him into his bed for the night.

"Go to sleep, my little vigilante, the defender of the commoners. You can fight off villains tomorrow when you feel better," he told him.

We were optimistic Zorro would soon be healthy, so we looked forward to the day when someone would adopt him. Zorro began healing, and we knew we could soon post him on our website. He had cast a spell on everyone who met him, charming them with his captivating personality and cute looks.

A week before he was to go on the website for adoption, Emmi noticed he had some new sores. We called Dr. Vincent to tell him and then had a volunteer drive Zorro to the clinic. When she got back to the shelter, she told us Dr. Vincent was putting him on a fresh round of antibiotics and a different ointment. We would also need to start his medicated baths again.

For the next two weeks, we treated Zorro as we had before. Trying to rule out anything that may cause the sores, I took him off any food containing chicken, thinking he might be allergic to it. We had discovered at the shelter that dogs with sensitive skin issues were often allergic to chicken. Two weeks went by with Zorro once again improving. The sores went away, and his hair started to thicken and look healthy.

A week later, I left for a four-day weekend, and when I returned to work, I found Zorro once again with open sores. Zorro's healing process was a source of frustration and confusion as the sores kept coming back. Once again, we placed a call to Dr. Vincent.

"You know," he said, "it's possible the shelter environment is causing him stress. I wonder if someone should take him home at night to see if it reduces the stress. My guess is he might get better in a normal home setting with his food monitored and his medications given on time every day."

I hadn't thought of taking him home, but it had been over two months since we had started his treatments, and I knew he had to get well before we could adopt him out.

That evening, I got all his things together, loaded him into my car, and started for home. As I was driving by Walmart, the thought struck me to go in and buy him an infant onesie. Inside the store, I picked out three, all in assorted boy colors and designs. When we arrived home, I wrestled him into one for his first fitting. Taking it off, I let him run around the house to get acquainted with his new surroundings and my dog. I rigged the onesies so they would fit him and not inhibit the bathroom process.

He looked adorable dressed up in his little outfit, and it did not seem to hinder him while he ran and played. I hoped this experiment would keep his sores clean, allowing his back to heal completely. He went into the play stance in front of my dog Jazzy, trying to get her to play with him. She was not interested and let him know she was the boss. As far as she was concerned, he was an enigma in a onesie. Not concerned by what she thought, he continued to bark and torment her, trying to coax her into a game of chase.

When my husband drove into the driveway, he could hear our new guest barking at him from the front step. With a look of surprise, he yelled from the pickup, "Who is the guy in the pajamas?"

"This is Zorro," I said. "He is our new guest."

He laughed harder as he got out of the pickup to greet him. "Zorro didn't wear PJs; he probably slept in the nude."

"Not funny!" I said, laughing. "I must admit, it's a unique experience to have a dog waiting for me at my front door in their PJs."

Little did he know that Zorro, wearing his onesie, was going to be a new passenger in his pickup, demanding to go with him on the morning rides.

It did not take long for Zorro to win my husband's heart. Zorro decided the dashboard was a great place to put his front paws as he watched for other dogs on their daily route. His little tail wagged in appreciation, thanking Mark for letting him ride along. The guys at the lumberyard would tease Mark, while Zorro, wearing his onesie, would confidently stand as if protecting my husband and his new territory—the pickup truck.

Laughing, they asked, "What is his name?"

"Zorro," my husband said.

Sipping their coffee, they commented, "Where did you come up with that name?"

"I would have named him Zippy," Bill said.

Mark tried to explain that Zorro was a character in a book who wore a black mask, and because the little dog had a black head, it looked like he was wearing a mask.

"My wife named him Zorro," he said, ready for the subject to change.

We found it amusing how most people did not know who the character Zorro was, suggesting they did not read or watch movies. Then one morning, one of the Hispanic yard workers came inside to get a fresh cup of coffee. Looking down at the barking dog in his blue onesie, he stood mesmerized, acting like he was seeing things. Meanwhile, Zorro continued to bark at him.

Carlos looked around the room at everyone. "Is this a joke? Who dressed this dog in a onesie?"

Looking at Mark, he then pointed at Zorro. "Is this your new dog?"

While Mark stood watching Carlos, he thought, here is someone who might know who Zorro was.

"Zorro, stop barking," Mark said.

"What did you call him?" Carlos laughed, a look of recognition on his face.

Mark smiled as he watched Carlos.

"His name is Zorro," he said again.

"Zorro!" Carlos said, dropping to one knee with respect while holding his hand to his heart.

Laughing, he continued, "El Zorro, come here. I am not a villain; of course, with your black head, which looks like a mask, what a perfect name for you." The other men who had been laughing at Zorro stopped to watch Carlos.

Carlos looked around at everyone, amused. "Zorro! Don't you know who Zorro was? He was a great man, a legend," he explained to them, waving his hands.

Leaning closer, he reached his hand out to pet Zorro. "But Mark, I do not understand; why does your wife put a onesie on the Zorro namesake?"

Mark leaned over to pick up Zorro and showed everyone his back, explaining to them. "Zorro has trouble healing from these sores, and my wife is hoping he will heal faster if he has something on to protect his back."

"I'm sorry I disrespected you, my friend," Carlos said, still laughing. "Do you want to carve a Z in my forehead?" Reaching out, he took Zorro from Mark, and speaking in Spanish, he said, "I am Carlos, your friend, and you are Zorro, the lover of my people."

Now that everyone at the lumberyard knew why Zorro was wearing a onesie, Mark knew the teasing would stop. On the mornings when Zorro did not come with him, they were concerned and asked about him.

Driving home, he started laughing. "Well, Zorro! Carlos knew who you were named after, and I think you have a larger fan club."

Zorro, in his onesie, with his front feet firmly planted on the dashboard, wagged his tail intently, watching for other dogs so he could defend his person and his pickup. After all, he is El Zorro.

Watching him, Mark laughed louder. "Yes, you are brave and courageous, even in a onesie, El Zorro."

Zorro did eventually get better, and one day, as he was

standing in his kennel, still wearing a onesie, he caught the eyes of two ladies. While he captivated them with his charm, they watched him through the window, oohing and aahing. They soon had him out and were sitting on the floor with him as he chased the toys they threw. Staff explained to them about his skin condition, and even though he seemed better, he might have more outbreaks.

Emmi shared with them his experience of being fostered and how he had healed nicely out of the shelter environment. The ladies were so enamored with him that Emmi was not sure they were listening until one of them looked up at her, and with tears running down her cheeks, said, "He reminds me of a dog we had with a skin condition a lot like this. We took him to the vet when his tummy would break out in sores, and the vet helped him get better every time."

Shaking the toy at Zorro, she continued, "He lived to be thirteen years old before we had to say a sad goodbye."

Looking at her sister sitting beside her, she asked, "Wasn't that right, Mary Margaret? We had him for thirteen years, didn't we?"

"Oh, at least thirteen years or maybe even fourteen," the other woman exclaimed. "I believe we did."

Standing there watching them, we knew Zorro could never find a better home than these two ladies. Zorro left that day with his two new friends, who would devote their lives to him, doting on and spoiling him. I knew he was in excellent hands, and I would never worry about him getting good food, medication, or vet care.

Once every two years, they would pay us a visit, with Zorro still charming and healthy. Then, suddenly, they did not come or call. I thought maybe Zorro had died, and it was too heartbreaking for them to come to the shelter to tell us. Then one day before I retired, I heard my director humming towards my office door.

"There is someone here to see you," she said in her singsong voice.

She stepped aside, and there was Zorro, held in the arms of his two companions. For a brief moment, I stood there in stunned silence before finding my voice to respond. "I thought maybe he had died."

"Died?" they responded in unison.

One sister looked at me indignantly, saying, "Not on our watch! He's got to stick around for a while; he has a closet full of clothes to wear."

We all laughed as I admired Zorro in his handsome plaid coat, with a matching bow tie attached to his collar. What a perfect retirement gift for me to see my little friend, now aging, but still in good health. I called him over, and he jumped onto my lap, giving me kisses. He still had his loving, charismatic personality, charming everyone he met.

When Zorro came into the shelter on that frigid January night, his skin issues were terrible. With the help of a skilled vet and the dedicated care of our staff, he made a remarkable recovery. Then, these two amazing ladies adopted him, and from that moment on, they cherished, pampered, and adored him beyond measure. He loved them back, bringing joy, love, and laughter to their home. They treated him like the prince he is, because, after all, he is:

El Zorro the courageous.

El Zorro the friend.

El Zorro the lover of his people.

"The world would be a nicer place if everyone had the ability to love as unconditionally as a dog."

M.K. CLINTON

JAZZY

The new year celebrations had come and gone, and I returned to work with the snow still on the ground. There had been about two weeks of snow over Christmas, and I was ready for some warmer weather. When I walked through the shelter doors, I heard the distinct, sharp bark of an Australian Cattle Dog, also known as the Blue Heeler. I quickly removed my coat and gloves and rushed to the dog kennels to find the Heeler.

In the first pod stood a male Aussie Heeler mix, and in the kennel beside him was the female, a beautiful Queensland. She was blue mottled with a red undercoat that ran down her legs, which were speckled with white freckles. When she looked up at me, I could see the white Bentley mark between her erect ears. She had a black patch that ran down over her left eye, giving her a comical look. This breed is intelligent, alert, loyal, and protective, which can make them cranky with strangers, but she seemed relaxed as she wagged her docked tail.

"Wow, where did you come from, my pretty girl?" I said.

I wanted to see what her reaction would be because of her breed, but after looking at me, she laid her head down on her front feet with a sigh. Hearing me, Kevin looked around the kitchen door.

"Oh, you found them," he said, smiling. "They came in New Year's Day; someone found them close to the shelter."

"Well, you are beautiful," I said to her.

Then, leaning over, I gazed into the other kennel. "And you are very handsome."

In the coming days, it surprised me when an owner did not call the shelter or come in to claim them. After seventy-two hours, they legally became ours to adopt out. A week later, I took the male, who they were calling Max, out to do his evaluation. Later in the afternoon, I took the female out, who they had named June. I walked her down to the laundry to get some bedding. While I was folding some blankets for the dog bed in my office, June smelled around the laundry room. She discovered the toy barrel, reached in, and picked out a favorite toy.

As I stood there watching her, I thought, "Hmmm! You look a little chubby to me."

I called her over to feel gently under her belly.

"What's going on in there, little girl? Do you have some babies growing?"

I leashed her up, and we walked back to the main building. Tapping on my director's door, she told me to come in.

"I think we are going to have puppies," I said, smiling.

My director looked over her glasses, sitting on the tip of her nose. "Will she bite if I try to examine her?" she asked.

"You never know with a Blue Heeler, but so far, she has been very gentle with everyone."

She came around her desk, bending over to place her hands beneath June's belly. As she felt around, we heard a soft growl. She quickly straightened up and walked back to her desk to sit down.

"Nope," she said. "She is just a little plump."

"I don't know," I said doubtfully. "She came in with a male."

"I have done this for many years, and I think I know when a dog is pregnant." She scolded me with a frown.

"Well, you're probably right; you have done this for a long time," I said, trying to appease her.

Picking up June's leash, I walked her back to her kennel. She crawled up onto her bed to lie down. I reached down, giving her a goodnight pet. As I stood there watching her, a gnawing feeling persisted, and I remained unconvinced that she wasn't pregnant.

Ten days later, on my day off, I got a phone call from my director.

"Well, I was right!" she trumpeted over the phone. "We have Blue Heeler puppies this morning."

There was a pause, and then she continued. "June must have had them last night or early this morning, but she won't let anyone come into the kennel with her to make sure everything is okay or to clean her up."

There was another silence at the other end of the line, and then she asked, "Would you be willing to come in today? You're the only one who might be able to handle her."

My first reaction was annoyance. I wanted to remind her I was the one who had thought June was pregnant, and she referred to her condition as being a little plump.

"Oh! So she was pregnant," I commented.

"Yes, yes," she sounded annoyed. "But we can't get into her kennel to check if everything is okay."

"How about if I come in around ten?" I said, still feeling put out.

"Oh, thank you, that would be great. I'll see you then." The other end of the line went dead. I put down my phone and threw my hands in the air, feeling exasperated, but soon my thoughts were on the puppies and June. Grabbing my coat, I left for the shelter.

As soon as I entered the dog runs, Pat approached me and began sharing the morning events.

"Boy, is June cranky!" she reported. "The director tried to go in with her this morning, but June tried to bite her, chasing her out of her kennel."

"Well, I will try to go in with her, but I don't want anyone coming around while I'm in there. I don't want her upset, and I don't want to get bit."

Pat crossed her arms in front of her, telling me she would stand guard at the door. Entering the kennel area, I quietly called June's name. I could hear the mewling sounds of her new puppies as they nursed. I looked in her kennel and could see June lying there with her new babies. When she heard my voice, her stub tail started thumping on the side of the bed.

"Hey, my friend," I breathed softly. "I hear you have puppies."

Carefully but confidently, I opened her door, keeping a close watch on her body language. She lay there watching me closely, and as I stepped inside, she stood up. Her puppies cried in protest at losing the warmth of her body and the nourishment from her nipples. She carefully stepped over them, walking over to greet me. I looked down on the rumpled blanket, counting three white puppies.

"Oh, they are beautiful, sweet girl," I said.

Slowly, I bent down, reaching out to touch one of them. June watched me, but she did not react, so I gently picked one up.

"A boy," I said, looking at his full, fat belly.

Gently, I laid him back down and picked up the next one.

"Another boy," I whispered quietly. "Wow, two boys. Let's have a look at this one."

The third one squirmed in my hand. "Oh, this one's a girl," I said.

"Well, June, you have two boys and a girl. Well done."

Reaching toward her, I scratched her behind her pricked ears. June wagged her tail as she showed off her babies. Now that I had my scent on them and she seemed relaxed with me handling them, I carefully removed the soiled bedding, replacing it with clean blankets. As I moved her puppies around, she seemed more nervous, jumping in and out of the bed, pushing my hands away, but she never tried to bite. I gave her fresh water and some food to eat. While she was eating, I stood there admiring her babies. Giving her a last pat, I turned off the lights and left the kennel area. I knew she was going to be a wonderful mom, so I left her to care for her new family. Walking to the front desk, I announced to everyone that we have two boys and a girl.

"Holy mackerel!" Pat exclaimed. "I can't believe June let you in with her. She was so ferocious with all of us this morning. She even tried to bite and chase." Before she could complete her sentence, our director's voice came.

"It is time to get back to work, everyone. This is Julie's day off, and I'm sure she has other things to do today."

After a moment of silence, I heard her say, "Julie, can you come into my office, please?"

I walked over to her office and leaned on the doorframe as she looked at me from behind her paper-strewn desk.

"Can we call you later if we need help with June?"

"Yes, I can come back," I answered her.

Then, almost in a whisper, she said, "I'm sorry. You were right about June."

"It's okay," I said, smiling. "We have a happy mom and three healthy puppies. Call me if you need me."

Waving, I turned and quietly shut her door.

Two days later, while I was cleaning the puppies, I noticed one of them did not look right. When I picked up the puppy, I noticed her right front leg was deformed and missing a significant portion of it. It looked like a fingery stub sticking out from her shoulder. I tucked her into my shirt and went to my director's office.

"Oh, oh," she said, turning her over in her hands.

"You are a little special one," she said, kissing the puppy on the nose.

"We will have to have that stump taken off as soon as she is old enough. We can start a special fund to raise the money for the surgery. I'll have Dr. Vincent look at it next time he comes in."

She kissed the puppy on the nose one last time, handing her back to me.

"Could you be here when he comes?" she asked. "I'm sure June will not let him near her brood."

"I'll make sure I'm here," I said as I left her office.

June did eventually let other staff members in with her babies, but she was cranky and did not put up with people trying to handle her pups too much. She had a special aversion to the squeegee, chasing staff out of the kennel when they had one in their hands, including me. She was careful with her special girl. As the boys grew, they would romp around wrestling and playing with each other, but if things got a little rough, June would pick up her crippled puppy, putting her back into the bed, making sure she was out of their way. When the puppies were six weeks old, we started telling the story of June's puppy, who needed surgery. We asked for help to raise the money for the amputation, and like so many of the shelter's wonderful donors, one man came forward offering to pay for the whole surgery. Now all we had to do was wait until they were weaned and ready for adoption.

The puppies kept growing, and soon it would be time for them to leave. Meanwhile, I was going through a personal crisis of my own. I am a hiker, and ten years earlier, I had found a puppy off a hiking trail. She screamed with fear as I carefully tucked her inside my coat so we could hike home. Calling my husband, I told him about her and asked him to bring home some puppy food. I then placed her in a laundry basket, covering it with a towel so she would feel safe. She was all black, small and petite, and looked like a miniature German Shepherd. It was obvious she was born in the woods, and this was her first human encounter, and she was terrified.

I took her to my vet to be examined. She told me she was around ten weeks old and some type of shepherd. Feeling her bony sides, she told me she was underweight and gave her a worm medicine. She told me to feed her a healthy puppy food so she could gain weight and thrive. My first thoughts were to socialize her and give her away to a suitable home, but before I could do that, I had to introduce her to the human world.

And so, our puppy project began, and with the help of my gentle lab and my husband, we slowly won her trust. She flourished under our care, but she remained distrustful of strangers. After a few weeks, I fell in love with her and knew I could not give her up, and named her Molly. Now, as a family member, she became the third party of our adventures and hiking excursions in the woods.

After Molly had been with us a few years, I noticed my older lab was rapidly showing her age. It was harder for her to hike, and the two dogs were changing roles, with Molly becoming the caretaker. Another year went by, and on a cool fall morning, Bailey died, leaving us to grieve, and with a grieving Molly. We continued on, the two of us hiking and exploring the trails of Little Mountain. Molly loved the hikes, soaking in the warm sun, smelling the wonderful woodlands she had been born in. When we came home, she laid by my feet, and at night beside my bed. Wherever I was, she was close by, always there, my loyal and faithful companion.

One day when Molly was nine years old, I noticed her breath was bad, so I took her to the vet, thinking she needed her teeth cleaned. Later in the day, as I was leaving to pick her up, a call came from the vet's office. He told me he had found a growth on her tongue, and it looked like cancer. We waited anxiously for the pathology report to come back. The test came back positive, confirming our fears. Molly had cancer. Sadly, the vet told me there was nothing he could do, and she had around six weeks to live. As the next six weeks passed, and her time was getting close, she could no longer eat and dropped weight. Her beautiful, black, silky coat became dull, losing its sheen. I would sit in front of her, wiping the drool that ran down her chest and legs, trying to keep her clean. I knew it was time, and I needed to let her go, so I did. My heart broke when I said goodbye to my girl, leaving me without a dog for the first time. For weeks after she was gone, I would listen for her or accidentally call her name. Everyone was trying to convince me to take one of June's pups, but I was still reaching my hand out at night towards Molly's bed to pet her.

The shelter readied itself for the adoption event of June's puppies. It was April, the air was fresh, and the tulips were blooming in the fields. The girl puppy had undergone amputation and spay a couple of weeks ago, and her recovery had been smooth. Her new home was with a vet tech who had worked with the shelter for many years. After being spayed and neutered, June and the boys were now eligible for adoption. Many applications came in on the boys. We carefully went through them, trying to decipher if the people had the knowledge and skills to take on the Heeler breed. We finally picked out two families and contacted them. Their adoption day finally arrived, and they both left with their new families.

That left June, and when I walked by her kennel that evening, she had her head down on her front paws, looking sad.

"Hey, beautiful girl," I said, opening up her kennel.

I walked in and sat down on the floor beside her. She got off her blanket and came over, laying down beside me, putting her head on my lap.

I ran my hand down her smooth coat. "Are you lonely?"

She snuggled closer.

"I'm lonely too," I said, as a tear dropped on her soft fur.

I sat there for a while, comforting her, stroking her back with my hand, feeling the warmth of her against my leg. I knew it was time to go home, but I just couldn't leave her behind. Standing up, I reached out of her kennel door to take down her leash, fastening it to her collar.

"Come on, June, let's go," I said.

We walked to the front desk. I pulled her paperwork from the dog book. Looking at my director, I said, "I'm taking her home."

She smiled. "I know! You two are meant to be together. She picked you as soon as she arrived at the shelter. We have been waiting for you to decide to take her home, so let's get the paperwork done."

June came home with me that day and brought healing to our grieving hearts. My husband and I initially named her Jazzy June, but we soon shortened it to Jazz. Jazz proved to be an ambassador to the Blue Heeler breed. Australian Cattle Dogs are one of the more intelligent dogs. Bred as a working dog, they possess high energy and drive. They are drovers, used mostly for cattle, but can work sheep as well. They have an uncanny knack for sizing you up, and will stubbornly submit to your leadership, but only if you exhibit true leadership. If you're not leading, they'll step in and get the job done. I've seen many owners make a command of their dog, and the dog will look at them as if to say, "Are you for real? I know what I'm supposed to be doing here."

Once trained, they are one of the most respected and error-free dogs you can have to work cattle. They are not a dog who want to socialize with people they do not know, or with other dogs. When the ranchers bring them to an event where they are working cattle, the dog will sit or lay feet forward, ears erect, intently watching, listening for instructions from their owner. Without training, they'll instinctively try to work the cattle and end up fighting with the other dogs. This causes a great deal of commotion, with the owners yelling at their untrained dogs. "You damn dog," they'll shout. "You get back here!"

This breed listens well, but if they think their owners have been unreasonable or disrespectful, they will drift away, crawling under a pickup in the shade to brood. If you could read his mind, I think the dog would say, "He can work his own damn cattle."

With proper training, these dogs are fun companions, making work easier and ranch life more enjoyable for their owners.

There is one more thing I need to mention with a Heeler: they love their pickups. It is the one thing they will guard with their life. I would never consider opening a pickup door with a Heeler sitting in the front seat. To the Heeler's way of thinking, it is a cardinal sin if you do, and they will make sure you never do it again. Jazzy was no different from any other Heeler I have ever met. As gentle as she was, she drew the line at the pickup door.

From the start, Jazzy was calm, reserved, and a true alpha. She controlled all dogs she met with a side glance. We could take her anywhere with her manners being impeccable. The Queensland Heeler fit her well, for she was a true queen. We always wondered who owned her before she came into our home. With any shelter dog, their past can be a mystery. If they are a great dog, people will try to guess what possibly could have happened that they ended up in an animal shelter. We were no different, wondering why no one came forward to claim such an exceptional dog.

Once in a while, we would see things which told us of her secret past. Like one afternoon while walking with my husband, a school bus approached. When it stopped to let children off, Jazzy sat down to wait, excitedly watching each child as if she expected a certain child to step down. When the child she was waiting for did not appear, she turned and came back to continue the walk. Children loved Jazz, and she loved children. She was always gentle with them, letting them pet her or lay beside her on the floor.

It didn't take long for us to understand why she ran away on New Year's Eve; she hated loud noise and fireworks. On the Fourth of July, she would go down to the dark recesses of the basement to hide, but because of her loyal nature, she would appear at the top of the stairs to check on us and make sure we were okay. We also discovered she was comfortable around piers, boats, and the water. She had her quirks around bikes or skateboards, and we had to watch her carefully. Being a true Heeler, she wanted to herd objects that moved quickly in front of her. She would resort to droving the grandchildren when they ran willy-nilly around the property.

Taking over Molly's spot by our bed, she joined my husband in the passenger seat of the pickup truck as he went about his daily rounds. She tolerated me if I had to ride along, grudgingly taking up most of the seat and making me sit in an uncomfortable position. She became my new hiking partner or spent her time at the gallery with my husband. I could bring her to work, and she would wander the dog kennels, letting me know when a dog was unbalanced. If she was concerned about a dog, she would lean on my leg, trying to push me away from them. When we adopted her, the vet thought she was around seven years old, and when she was around eleven, we introduced another Australian Shepherd Border mix into her life so she could help us train him. At thirteen, she slowed down, having less energy. Her walks became slower, and it became an effort for her to go on hikes or to work with my husband.

We still hung onto our precious girl, but then one day she stopped. She would not eat or get up. We knew she was saying goodbye, and it was her time to go. My devoted, loyal girl needed to leave us, and once again, we grieved. I can't help but wonder why we do this to ourselves, but if we didn't, we'd miss out on the love and companionship of dogs, and that would be such a major part missing from our lives. To have a dog is to have a loyal friend who loves you completely, a teacher, a gift from God. Edith Wharton wrote, "My little dog—a heartbeat at my feet."

I am dedicating this book to Jazzy because everyone should have a dog like her. She was a loyal friend and came into my life when I needed her—and she needed me.

I read a quote once by an unknown author which said, "Dogs leave a paw print on our hearts."

Jazzy left her paw print on mine.

ACKNOWLEDGMENTS

To Janine, Erika, Tiffany, Annie, Eileen, Jane, Jarin, Kim, Christina, Veronica, my co-workers, and so many others who dedicate their lives and hearts to animals, working tirelessly to improve the well-being of those in their care—thank you.

To the beloved volunteers—Cindy, Lucy, John, Debbie, Debra, Jannet, Mackenzie, Dianna, David, and countless more—who give so much of their time walking dogs and caring for all the animals at the shelter, your compassion knows no bounds.

To all the wonderful people I've met who opened their hearts and homes to adopt a dog and give them a second chance, you are truly making a difference.

To the veterinarians, vet techs, and their staff, who work tirelessly to care for shelter animals, your dedication is beyond measure.

To the animal control officers and police officers, who are often the first responders in tragic situations involving animals, thank you for the difficult work you do.

To the Boeing K9 program, for seeking out working dogs from shelters and training them for service, your efforts change lives.

To our Vietnam Veterans, and to all the men and women who serve our country, I offer my deepest gratitude.

To my husband, thank you for listening to my writing and encouraging me to keep going.

To my mom, Georgia; my children, Kim, Melynda, and Lance; my sister, Linda; and my brothers, John and David, thank you for your unwavering support and love.

To Cameron, our family historian, thank you for helping me find Grandpa Wilson's World War I records.

To John and Kim Knoernschild, thank you for your invaluable advice and for introducing me to my editor.

Thank you, Marion, from Seaport Books, for your guidance and encouragement.

Finally, to my editor, Julie Pershing, for your hard work and expertise, a big thank you.

~ Julie Bistranin

ABOUT THE AUTHOR

Julie Bistranin was raised in the Shields Valley of rural Montana. Surrounding herself with animals, she easily joined their natural world. Her grandfather taught her that animals were teachers, and we journey through life with them. He had a special gift with horses, passing down this gift to Julie, but her passion was with dogs. Their behaviors, pack mentality, loyalty, and natural inclination to please drew her in, making them easy to  train. She studied dogs to understand their thinking and the characteristics of different breeds, so she could train them to reach their full inherent potential.

After moving to Washington, she served fifteen years working at her local animal shelter, where she focused on evaluating, correcting behavior problems, and training. Helping dogs become better behaved, find loving homes, or be placed in suitable working situations was a source of great honor for Julie. Since retiring, she dedicates her time to writing and lives in Mt Vernon, Washington, with her husband, Mark.

How You Can Help:
Leave a Review!

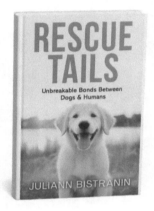

If you enjoyed *Rescue Tails*, I would be so grateful if you would take a moment to leave a positive review on Amazon.

Your feedback, no matter how brief, helps more readers discover the magic of these stories and supports the work of independent authors.

Thank you for being part of this adventure and for helping me continue to write books that make a difference.

Your Journey Begins Here...

Turn Your Passion into a Published Book

Bring your book to life—connect with us today!

hello@gallivantpress.com
www.gallivantpress.com

Made in United States
Troutdale, OR
11/19/2024

25037979R00116